THE VOLUNTEER TRAVELER'S HANDBOOK

How to find ethical and sustainable international volunteer opportunities.

Shannon O'Donnell

The Volunteer Traveler's Handbook: How to find ethical and sustainable international volunteer opportunities.

© Copyright 2012 by Shannon O'Donnell

ISBN 978-0-9877061-4-0

ISBN 978-0-9877061-4-0

Cataloguing data available from Library and Archives Canada

Disclaimer:

This book provides entertaining and informative snapshots of the writer's personal experiences and helpful tips from the writer and others, learned while volunteering and traveling around the world. The tips provided in this book are not meant to serve as an exclusive checklist to effectively safeguard the reader in every travel situation. Each reader should complete updated, detailed research from legitimate sources to learn the cultural norms and safety recommendations for their specific destination. No one can guarantee safety and travel can expose everyone to potential risks. Because safety is impacted by each person's actions and choices, each reader is advised to always do their homework on their destination and use their best judgment while on their journey.

I wish you safe, happy and fulfilling travels.

To the people I met at each stage of my travels,
and in each place I volunteered.

For your stories.
For your lessons.
Simply, thank you.

Acknowledgements

Much a testament to the nature of travel, throughout the months writing this book, it slowly came to life as I traveled in Thailand, Burma, and Cambodia. The book was then fine-tuned in Florida, Oregon, Washington, and Virginia. And if the eclectic collection of places is any indication of the thanks due, there are many people who helped shape the ideas and stories within.

A thank you to my dad for his support of my ongoing travels, and to both my parents for the welcoming hugs each time I return home. And to my niece Ana, thank you for bringing light and joy to our trip together. Friends often bridge the gap into family; heartfelt thanks to: Stephanie, Niki, Niki, Jenn, J.J. and Joanne.

And thank you to the travelers who have impacted my life in ways too numerous to count. Jodi, you are a sister from a past life; thank you for your friendship and sage advice every step of the way. Dan and Audrey, your feedback was both timely and invaluable—thank you. And to Dani and Jess, a thanks for your friendship and your help with my niece Ana while I drafted this book in Cambodia.

Thanks to each volunteer and traveler who shared a story in this book. And a final thank you to Janice Waugh, I appreciate your guidance and support and for the chance to share my stories as a part of this series.

Contents

Contents

The Backstory

Throughout my college years, I was motivated to tackle life with a rosy idealism and sincere commitment to serve my community. I joined almost any volunteer project that crossed my path. I raised funds annually for the American Cancer Society, served breakfast to the homeless in my city, and volunteered at my local animal shelter. The opportunities were there, and I had the time and desire to serve.

Fast-forward to my post-university life, however, and somehow I found myself bogged down with personal daily dramas that preoccupied my days. I moved from my home state of Florida to Los Angeles, California after graduation and I lost all my focus on service and volunteering. And, though only partly correlated, I found myself less happy with life in general.

In 2008, after two years in Los Angeles, I felt an urge to change my life to embrace a dream I had always nurtured but had never expressed. I decided to pack up my life and travel around the world for a year.

But this time I wouldn't lose my focus. I would volunteer. I would bring serving others back into my life. Not as my primary focus, but rather as a regular complement to how I live and travel. With that in mind, I promised myself I would find and work on service-based projects whenever the opportunity presented itself as I traveled.

Over the course of my one-year trip, word of mouth brought me to a well-run orphanage on the outskirts of Phnom Penh, Cambodia. The orphanage was filled with motivated, bright students in a loving environment where all their needs were being met.

My sense of fairness took me to restaurants and shops operating with a social mission: a café using money to train street kids, a restaurant-cum-school teaching the local refugee community the languages and skills they needed to excel outside their home country.

In 2009, my love of children brought me to a monastery in Pharping, Nepal, where I taught English language classes for 46 young monks in a small town one hour outside of Kathmandu. That month impacted my life in many ways —and likely more than my time impacted any of those children.

I found the monastery through a middleman organization—a placement company that matches volunteers with projects for a fee. That side of my volunteer experience tanked for many reasons. What it boils down to, and the main lesson that I learned, was that I didn't ask the right questions. I didn't ask where my placement fee was going, and didn't know enough at the time to really make sure that the middlemen had the best interests of the community at the heart of their work.

I feel incredibly fortunate that the issues with the placement organization did not prevent me from working with my students. No, that part was fantastic. But the sum of the experience opened my eyes to another side of the volunteering industry that I, in my naiveté, had never considered.

With that experience to fuel me over the next three years as I continued traveling, I worked on my passion project: a community-sourced database of independent volunteer opportunities, philanthropic businesses, and social enterprises located all over the world. It took years to crystallize the idea. And as I formed the site GrassrootsVolunteering.org, it occurred to me that more was needed. That *beyond* the database, there was an entire side of volunteering abroad that I hadn't understood until I spent years on the road talking to people, organizations, and other volunteers.

The Volunteer Traveler's Handbook is my "beyond." It's the other side of the volunteer industry that every volunteer and socially responsible traveler should understand. It's the missing pieces, the questions you never thought to ask. Travelers of any age, any background, and any travel style can find a way to give back to the communities they visit. But how travelers give back can vary greatly. It can mean using fair-trade retail shops, restaurants, and spas in a new city. It can mean reducing the negative environmental footprint of travel by participating in conservation projects. And it definitely means understanding the ethical side of the volunteering industry so volunteers can pick projects and opportunities fit for both the local community and the volunteer's goals.

My purpose in writing this handbook started as a seed of an idea in 2009 when I taught in Nepal. I wasn't aware of the social and community impact my volunteer choices made back then, and my sole goal is to give you, the traveler, the tools you need to make positive choices as you travel the world.

The rowdy class of kindergarten children race to answer questions in class at the Manjushri Di-Chen Learning Center in rural Nepal.

LAYING THE GROUNDWORK

"Each person's task in life is to become an increasingly better person."
Leo Tolstoy

Projects and Learning with Children in Cambodia

A slow whirling ceiling fan circulated the lazy, heat-drenched air as my friend Laura and I prepared our lesson plans. I had arrived at the Future Light Orphanage (FLO) in Phnom Penh, Cambodia just one week prior, and I had spent the week reading with children in the library and assisting the teachers in the orphanage's development skills classes.

Images from TV commercials that I had seen while growing up in the United States had given me all sorts of preconceptions about Cambodia, ideas that I took into my travels and volunteering in the country. But each day volunteering at FLO provided experiences that defied these stereotypes. Though many children were, in fact, orphans, they were far from destitute and lonely. The orphanage was run more like a boarding school; each child attended the local public school full-time while attending additional skills development classes hosted by FLO.

I visited FLO as a short-term volunteer. This is actually something I don't recommend when volunteering with children, but I was too naïve at the time to realize the potential dangers. FLO is a well-run orphanage, but there are many Cambodian orphanages lacking any oversight of interactions between volunteers and children.

At FLO, the 200 children share a huge compound and each dorm is run by long-term den mothers who take care of the children's schedules and needs. Short-term volunteers are encouraged to work on small projects with the older children; the older children are considered less vulnerable.

On my first day at FLO, I was very unsure of where I could fit in with the schedule and volunteer activities. Volunteering is an add-on to life at FLO, not the point of the orphanage. To help us find a way to serve, Laura and I were encouraged to talk with Bunyap, the English language teacher for FLO's teens. At Bunyap's suggestion, we supplemented his existing lessons with a song aimed at motivating the kids to learn new vocabulary, and getting them excited to practice English pronunciation.

Laura and I brainstormed on our first day and really thought about which song was slow enough to sing along with, but had a good beat and meaningful lyrics. Naturally, we taught the group a rousing rendition of "Lean on Me" by Bill Withers and we were rewarded with hilarious enactments and melodrama as they sang.

Each of the eight days I spent at FLO, I worked on mini-projects. These projects assisted the teachers as much as the children, as the teachers could continue implementing our lesson plans and projects long after Laura and I left Cambodia. My week at FLO was my first introduction to teaching English as a foreign language and I learned how Bunyap tailored English lessons to keep his teens interested. From FLO, I took away a deeper compassion for the children working so hard, every day, for the chance to have a decent education.

FLO also taught me that no lasting change made in the world is accomplished alone. I did not change that orphanage in any tangible way. But I was able to spend a few afternoons tutoring Bunyap on his pronunciation, which will, hopefully, leave a tiny, lasting improvement to his ability to teach and empower his students.

The students at FLO are trained to become the future leaders of Cambodia, according to the organization's founder. Each child is given more education and skills than the public education system can currently provide, in the hopes that English and computer skills will help them attain higher paying jobs once they graduate.

While at FLO I became Facebook friends with at least six of the teens—their caregivers cleared the connection—and to this day I frequently chat with some of them, keeping tabs on their university studies and new jobs and lending advice when they ask. Many students have gone on to work in finance, politics, and education. Volunteering allowed me to make this connection, and to watch these children grow and change over the years.

Exploring jungle pathways to the ruined temples of Angkor Wat brought history to life, and complemented my volunteer time in Cambodia.

What is International Volunteering?

Volunteering means different things to different people. At its most basic, volunteering encompasses all experiences where you donate your time, skills, and abilities to help an organization further its social cause. Unparalleled global interconnectedness over the last decade has allowed more and more travelers to look for ways to add volunteer experiences to their vacations.

The two main sectors of the mainstream international volunteering industry include independent volunteering and voluntourism through tours/ middlemen.

On the margins of volunteering is social enterprise, which is rarely included with volunteering. I think it belongs there nonetheless. Social enterprise is a relatively new term increasingly being used in development circles to refer to organizations that are advancing a social mission though more traditional business means. These enterprises earn income and operate as businesses, but implement a social, environmental, or community-driven mission. For travelers, this means that you can spread funds to various causes and businesses—and thus, various local families—in a more direct, grassroots manner.

We'll touch on the pros and cons of each of these volunteer sectors later and discuss when to support social enterprises. For now, let's look at the various volunteer experiences available.

Types of Volunteering Experiences Include:

- teaching/education
- disaster relief support
- environmental
- agriculture and farming
- medical and healthcare
- child-based programs
- conservation
- community development
- humanitarian
- office work
- marketing
- programming and coding

Types of Social Enterprises that Need Your Support:

* restaurants
* retail shops
* artisans
* bakeries

* tailors
* craft centers
* local tour operators

Far from comprehensive, this is a sample of the places that benefit from local, grassroots support from travelers. Depending on your background, your unique skills and passions are likely in demand somewhere in the world. Or, your tourist dollars can go to support shops and businesses with a strong social purpose. No matter your perceived limitations, there are worthwhile, ethical opportunities if you're keen to do a bit of research first.

Who Should Volunteer and Travel Sustainably?

If you're reading this handbook, then it's likely you. And you're not alone.

Statistics show that an increasing number of travelers are looking for vacations that support local communities. Since 2002, the number of volunteer vacations has more than doubled according to a *Condé Nast Traveler*/MSNBC survey,[1] while a 2008 research study by Tourism Research and Marketing surveyed 300 organizations and estimated the market size to be 1.6 million volunteer tourists per year. That same study valued the market at roughly $2 billion.[2] I anticipate this number will continue to grow as more information, opportunities and resources are available to travelers.

So, who are these travelers? Who is out there responsibly supporting local communities and practicing sustainable tourism? Volunteer travel experiences are as varied as the places and people on this planet. Not every experience is right for each person, but each interested traveler can find just the right way to give back and support local communities while traveling.

Who Chooses Service Oriented Vacations?

- vacationers
- career breakers
- families
- long-term travelers
- solo travelers
- traveling couples
- college students
- career professionals

- midlifers
- seniors
- teens
- introverts
- extroverts
- wealthy travelers
- budget travelers
- religious groups

People from all walks of life seek out the transformative power of travel and service. If you have a keen desire for new experiences and the fresh perspective that comes from traveling, then international volunteering will likely be a very rewarding personal choice.

Vibrant colors and ornate costumes adorn these elephants in Jaipur, India as a way to welcome the coming spring during Holi, an annual festival held throughout many parts of South Asia.

Benefits to the Volunteer

Let's face it, although there is much selflessness involved in volunteering (your gift of time, money, and effort), it also directly benefits you, the volunteer, in many positive ways. High on the list of personal volunteering benefits is satisfaction from the experience of giving. Many of these benefits apply to international volunteering in particular. Domestic volunteering has many similar benefits, however, which can be achieved when you choose to travel and serve in your home community. Let's look at the top motivating factors for many volunteers.[3]

Build Your Résumé. Volunteering in your field of study strengthens your understanding of global issues related to your topic and looks great when you apply for jobs. As companies globalize, they look for applicants who understand sensitive international cultural issues.

Engage in Real-Life Internships. Like the résumé-builder, but this time for course credit or advanced thesis work.

Gain Deeper Cultural Understanding. Volunteers often work directly with local communities for days and weeks at a time, learning pieces of the language and culture that go far below the surface. If you volunteer domestically, you may discover pockets of culture quite different from your hometown.

Develop Interpersonal Communication Skills. Post-volunteer feedback indicates that volunteers feel that their ability to articulate ideas and communicate with others increased after long-term volunteer experiences.

Use a Home Base for Exploring a Region. Staying in one location allows you to really explore the region surrounding your volunteer project. Starting with a volunteer experience can make independent travel to nearby cities easier and more rewarding.

Foster Friendships. You'll often work closely with other volunteers, building a common bond and shared experience. This is particularly a plus for solo travelers volunteering internationally.

Improve Problem Solving Skills. At its very root, the act of travel forces you to learn creative ways to problem solve. Volunteering, similarly, will stretch your mind as you find new solutions.

Share Your Skills. Use your skills to empower, teach, and share on projects directly related to your field. Match yourself with an organization working with local communities to pass on the specialized knowledge.

Develop New Skills. Both skilled and unskilled volunteer placements will likely have you partaking in activities you've never experienced before.

Volunteering at Habitat for Humanity with several friends after we jointly attended a conference in Portland, Oregon.

Did You Know?

Research indicates that volunteers experience less depression, live longer, and enjoy a host of other benefits at least partly because they spend time in service to others. This evidence points to the social integration aspect of volunteering as the root cause of such rewards.[4]

According to researcher Ariel Garten, we are pre-programmed to foster connectedness with others.[5] She notes that pro-social behavior is wired into our brains from birth, that an individual "not only care[s] about their own utility but take[s] the utility of others into account."[6] In my mind, it fits with the fact that survival in the past relied on our ability to not only keep ourselves alive, but also to keep each member of our community alive.

Serving your own community and giving back has positive personal, mental, and health benefits over a lifetime. Several prominent research studies find direct and fairly immediate benefits for older volunteers, while college-age and midlife volunteers see those same benefits when they practice regular community service.[7]

Analyze Why You Want to Volunteer

Your internal motivations for volunteering are as important as the volunteer experience itself. Ask yourself these questions and write down your responses. You are the only person who will ever see the answers, so be open and honest about your motivations for volunteering. I consulted with Laura Carroll, an independent student researcher at the Planeterra Foundation, on how volunteers can delve deeper and discover their root motivations. The idea here is to gain perspective, keep your ego in check, and have a clear picture of what you bring to the organizations.

What are my skills?

What are my goals?

What are my motivations?

What are my assumptions?

What do I hope to give?

What do I hope to gain?

What essential elements must a volunteer program have for me?

What kind of a difference do I want to make in the world?

Am I willing to listen to people who are different from me?

How do I react to criticism? What actions can I take to ensure that I accept and work with constructive criticism when I volunteer?

What assumptions and expectations about volunteering do I hold right now?

❝ *While I have volunteered my time and skills with many projects in the past, I mostly chose instead to fundraise. Because I travel permanently, there are issues around physical proximity, Internet connections and time zones that make it hard for me to give my best to a volunteer position. Fundraising is usually less dependent on those factors, so it's much easier for me to make a significant contribution in that way. Right now, I serve as one of the unofficial faces of One Girl's "Do It in a Dress" campaign. The idea to fundraise for One Girl was born out of a conversation I had with one of the founders. I share the campaign via blogs and social media and actively promote and fundraise throughout the year in a variety of ways that usually involve me doing embarrassing things in a girl's school uniform. I wear a school dress so a school-aged girl in Sierra Leone, Africa can wear one too with the funds I have raised.* **❞**

Dave Dean
WhatsDaveDoing.com

Understand Your Effect on People and Places

At this point, you are likely psyched and ready to volunteer, right? You've dreamed of helping out somewhere, taking a vacation and giving back. You love the benefits you'll get and your heart is in the right place. Now let's take a look at the ethical landscape of volunteering so you're bringing the maximum amount of help to the right projects and the right organizations.

Not every organization is doing good work.

Right off the bat, understand that some organizations may truly believe that they are coming from a positive place of giving and help, when in fact they are not. Organizations must consider the needs of the community and the long-term impact of voluntourism on both the local ecosystem and the people directly and indirectly affected by volunteering efforts. For this book, we will call those people affected by your efforts the voluntoured. If the affected people and places are not fully included in the volunteer process, then an organization may be doing more harm than good. Also, some organizations exploit local natural resources to fund projects, but never mention this detail.

In the worst case scenarios, there's not even the guise of naiveté, and an organization is simply skilled at masking the fact that they're in it for profit rather than culturally sustainable development.

It's also worth noting upfront that much of this ethics section centers on volunteer experiences working with people, as opposed to ones working with the environment. That being said, there are countless conservation and animal welfare projects that have similar issues at their core. If you're focused on working with plants or animals, rather than directly with people, it's still important to read this ethics section. It is every volunteer's responsibility to make sure their chosen organization is working toward fixing the right types of problems, in a way that respects and includes local cultures and communities.

Abu Abdullah used a mortar and pestle to grind fresh cardamom and coffee, a traditional welcome drink in Jordan. Abu lives in Wadi Feynan and while I visited, I spent the afternoon listening to his stories about the Bedouin community's culture and heritage.

Psychology and Ethics of Volunteering

Before working in any volunteer capacity, you should first consider the issues of dignity and dependence.

Does the organization (be it an independent local company or a major voluntour operator) center their programs on maintaining the dignity of every person in the community?

Is the organization responding to the community's specific and communicated needs (not perceived needs) and empowering them toward a long-term, sustainable community that is not dependent on international volunteers to thrive?

The ultimate sense of security will be when we come to recognize that we are all part of one human race. Our primary allegiance is to the human race and not to one particular color or border.

Mohamed ElBaradei, International Atomic Energy Agency

Maintaining Dignity

There is often an overlooked side effect of volunteering that positions the volunteer as a benevolent helper to the voluntoured. This situation is termed "othering" in research studies within the academic community.[8] The volunteer wants to do service and feel good, and often, that good feeling is born out of direct contact with the voluntoured. But, the researchers ask, how do the voluntoured feel when you spend a weekend in their community handing out your used clothes?

And what about the wrenching relationships children form with short-term volunteers at orphanages? Some short-term volunteers want to play with and hug orphans, to see their plight and maybe read them a story. Then the volunteers leave, feeling like their afternoon has "done some good for the world," while the children are left waiting to temporarily bond with the next batch of good Samaritans.

In each of these situations, the volunteering circumstances compromise the dignity of the locals.

To better understand, think about the alternatives. In the first circumstance, volunteers could build a community system to employ locals and orchestrate skills training. Then, the community could perhaps purchase those same used clothes at a thrift store. Handouts from volunteers and travelers leave the voluntoured indebted to the foreigners and dependent on their handouts. But buying those same clothes for a nominal, regionally appropriate fee empowers the community toward self-sufficiency.

As for orphan tourism, this is a huge global issue right now, with Africa being a front-runner for afternoon playdates. In many cases, tours drop off travelers for mere hours so they can hug orphans with AIDS. Travelers then get back on their tour bus feeling good about themselves.[9] These children have become objects and only serve to reinforce stereotypes in many ways. Short-term projects involving children and volunteers are often flawed and should be well researched before you participate.

Eliminating Dependency

Unemployment is a global problem, and a problem that affects you as a potential volunteer. Volunteer programs walk a fine line between adding needed skills, time, and labor to a community and taking jobs that could benefit locals. Even some community-developed projects may not have considered the issue of long-term dependency during the planning stages. In many cases communities are desperate to infuse cash into the local economy with voluntourism fees, which leads to poorly planned volunteer projects.

Organizations using volunteers to build houses, schools, and painting projects are fine on the surface. The community needs a school, and your labor helps build it, right? They need eye exams, so isn't it ideal that doctors volunteer for weeks and months to examine a community?

In the building situation, hiring local labor would invest the money donated for the volunteer project directly into the community. So it is clearly ideal to hire local labor, right? Well, this is where the web gets tangled when we're talking about volunteering. Often, the fees and donations from volunteers actually fund these projects. Communities bring in volunteers as a way to raise those needed funds, and that's not a bad idea for them either.

The crux of the issue is that some programs create a system that can only be maintained by more volunteering and foreign donations. This is dependency. This is not ideal because it keeps foreigners as the support system for a community. The United Nations and other global groups are finding ways to empower local economies to grow and thrive without continued money and support.

There are examples of the dependency issue within each field. Medical students offering treatments are a wonderful short-term fix, but add training to the mix and you have a long-term solution at the local level. Raising funds and constructing a school is surely good, but working with the community to set up a system that can support a school with teachers and supplies over several decades is better.

Room to Read is a wonderful example of an organization working on literacy *with* communities across Asia and Africa. Room to Read builds libraries and school literacy programs in collaboration with local communities and governments. Each community provides a half monetary co-investment in the project, which ensures the community wants and needs the library or school and has a vested interest in maintaining the project over the long term.

Perhaps the easiest way to illustrate this point is to fall back on this eloquent and succinct fishing parable:

"Give a man a fish and you feed him for a day; teach a man to fish, and you feed him for a lifetime."

Even if you plan to volunteer in the United States, United Kingdom, Europe, Australia, or any westernized and developed country, this idea of dependency is a challenge in building lasting change. And it's certainly an important issue to consider in the creation of sustainable improvements in the developing world. Teach people how to fish. Teach a homeless man construction in the West, or a woman from Africa how to sew and sell trinkets. Or perhaps train a new mom in nursing skills so she can ensure her village's long-term health. Many volunteer programs could benefit from prioritizing training so skilled volunteers are able to leave that knowledge behind.

For dependency, the middle ground lies within training and collaboration. Organizations aimed at decreasing long-term dependency through skills training and empowerment, in conjunction with volunteer placements, are ideal.

Why Should You Understand The Two Ds?

Please think about every angle of a potential volunteer experience. For many volunteers, the issues of dependency and dignity give a new perspective on volunteering. I point it out here so you can approach your research with as much information as possible.

Next up we will examine company structure and other ways you can vet volunteer organizations. But through it all, I want you to have a well-balanced perspective on the real-life effects—both positive and negative—that volunteering can have on the very real people and places you are hoping to help.

In the next section we'll look at questions you can ask your potential organizations to suss out if their programs consider The Two Ds. Start thinking now, though, about volunteer project descriptions you may have already encountered in your research, and process them with this dependency and dignity model in mind.

All human beings are born free and equal in dignity and rights.
They are endowed with reason and conscience and should act
towards one another in a spirit of brotherhood.
Article 1. in the Universal Declaration of
Human Rights by the United Nations

Locally employed women run the House of Calligraphy in Rasun, Jordan; they teach the culture, history, and technique behind classic Arabic script.

An Essay on the Delicate Balance in Volunteering
Laura Carroll works with travel and tourism companies on sustainable international development models.

In my study of Sustainable International Development, one of the things driven home to me time and time again, is that the road to hell really is paved with good intentions. Over the past several decades, any number of development projects have failed, sometimes leaving the target communities worse off than before. The concept of "development" itself can be problematic, and contains vestiges of colonialism—after all, most models for development have the underlying assumption that all countries should eventually follow the model of the US and Western Europe. There's a delicate balance that needs to be struck in development work, between helping people in the ways that make sense to us as outsiders and helping people in the ways they really need.

During my eight months in Egypt working with the Planeterra Foundation, my role was to identify and evaluate projects for the foundation to work with. This work was connected to my Master's Degree and followed a year of intensive international development coursework, so I came to Egypt with all sorts of ideas about "perfect" sustainable development projects. I was going to find the best damn project the world had ever seen, Planeterra would fund it, travelers would visit it, and it would be glorious.

Once I got to Egypt, though, I quickly discovered that "perfect" projects simply didn't exist there. Egypt has some of the strictest NGO laws in the world, which means that civil society in the country has been extremely curtailed. There were small local charities and large internationally-funded projects, but there was very little in between. I knew Planeterra wanted to work with smaller projects that hadn't attracted the attention of major aid organizations. But as I looked at the small-scale, community-organized projects I was finding, I didn't initially recognize how special they were, because they didn't fit the development project models I had been taught in school.

It took stepping back and looking at these projects within their context—rural Egypt just a few months after the revolution—for me to understand just how amazing many of them were. Once I'd figured it out, I was able to make my recommendations to Planeterra. Through my research, the foundation supported three new projects in Egypt. One of them, the Todd Community Education Center, will even be visited by G Adventures tours.

I share this story because it shows that even with the best will in the world, even with a degree in development and a mind I thought was completely open, I still had preconceived notions of what I was going to find in Egypt. Those notions actually limited me in the work that I was able to do there. As I settled into Egypt, I balanced my knowledge of sustainable development with local knowledge of Egypt around the time of the revolution.

Balance is hard to find, no matter how much I had prepared, no matter how much I thought I knew beforehand.

Managing Expectations and Perspectives

You alone will not change the world.

It's a blunt statement, but it's true and we should acknowledge it upfront.

The old colonial era attitudes have mostly shifted, and on the surface we realize the value of allowing cultures to thrive and embrace their differences. Below the surface, however, there have been some huge blunders in the past several decades as individuals and organizations brought in outside ideas, thought patterns, and solutions to communities that neither needed nor wanted the changes.

There have also been incredible successes all over the world, where people have taken one idea and created a positive impact on a local community, ecosystem, or culture. Projects using crowdsourcing to pool together resources have impacted numerous volunteer initiatives.

Expectations, though, are a huge pitfall for successful volunteering. At the root of many unsuccessful volunteering experiences is extreme disappointment when the volunteer expected noticeable and instant transformation.

Development projects anywhere in the world need consistent and long-term partnerships to realize any identifiable change.

The best example I can give to help you set your expectations for change comes from looking at the history of the Peace Corps, an American organization run by the US federal government. The organization launched in 1961, and since that time has allowed Americans to serve in more than 130 countries around the world. The Peace Corps is not lacking in critics; there are many who feel the organization has seen little lasting change or positive international development from its programs.

But that's far from the truth. The organization is in this for the long-term. For decades. Some projects and communities will receive several decades of support and Peace Corps development projects before any measurable "success" is achieved. Each member of the Peace Corps commits to two years of service with the organization.

That commitment term means most volunteers leave their volunteer service having seen only a tiny fraction of the project or development work completed within that community. This is normal even outside of the Peace Corps; most major development organizations have ten- to twenty-year plans for the work they complete.

Now let's talk about attitude. Your attitude and willingness to listen and learn about your new community directly correlates to your volunteer enjoyment. Whether you're volunteering internationally or domestically, understand what your volunteer commitment means in the broad scale of the project's aim. It could mean you leave your volunteer placement having added just one block to the pyramid still to be built. But if the next person steps up, volunteers, and places the next block—and the next, and the next—well, that's when real and lasting change happens.

Traveling makes one modest — you see what
a tiny place you occupy in the world.
Gustave Flaubert

Building stoves in the rural areas outside of Xela, Guatemala gives villagers an alternative to the dangerous open cooking fires they traditionally use inside their homes.

Why is the Developing World ... Developing?

There is no earthly way I could provide adequate coverage on this topic in this handbook. Countless people have theorized on development issues over the years: researchers, novelists, economists, ethnographers, anthropologists, and historians, just to name a few. Many of these people are far more qualified than me.

I can say, though, that there are far more factors involved than you have likely ever considered unless you regularly follow this topic. Assumptions kill the truth and lead to uninformed travel. The tapestry of issues separating a "developing" nation from a "developed" one is complex and interwoven with cultural, natural, environmental, and political influences. Access to natural resources, politics, the role of the military, a lack of free markets, overpopulation, human rights issues, and government structure are just a few pieces of the puzzle.

Some good academic reads on the subject include:

Uncharitable: How Restraints on Nonprofits Undermine Their Potential by Dan Pallotta

The Bottom Billion: Why the Poorest Countries are Failing and What Can Be Done About It by Paul Collier

Development as Freedom by Amartya Sen

The Elusive Quest for Growth: Economists' Adventures and Misadventures in the Tropics by William R. Easterly

Portfolios of the Poor: How the World's Poor Live on $2 a Day by Daryl Collins

Useful websites and magazines:

Mother Jones: motherjones.com
Nonprofit news specializing in social justice reporting.

Chris Blattman: chrisblattman.com
An academic on political economic theory and development.

Blood and Milk: bloodandmilk.org
Alanna Shaikh delves deep into a range of international issues.

From Poverty to Power: oxfamblogs.org/fp2p/
Duncan Green debates and discusses development policies.

A Rabbit Hole in Media Stereotypes

The media, news, television dramas, and films have distorted our perceptions of what developing nations and their people are really like.[10] The core of sustainable travel (volunteering and supporting local businesses) is the ability to gain global perspectives and eliminate the stereotypes perpetrated and perpetuated by the media.

Realities and Perceptions of Developing Nations

Perception	Reality
Living in abject poverty	Many places have a wealthy elite, or even a growing middle class alongside abject poverty. Not every place is defined solely by its poverty.
Very different from us	People's everyday concerns and worries are the same i.e., jobs, family, food, and children.
Living in the past	Modern technology and traditional customs combine in most places. Cell phones are prevalent all over the world and satellite technology brings the Internet and forms of modernization to even remote places.
Victims	The will to help themselves and be self-sufficient is a high priority for many communities when asked.
Lazy	People work much harder there just to exist as there is no government support system.

If the only thing you get is the negative stories, you become inured and people seem less human—they are either emaciated victims or violent and evil.
Dr David Keen

Burmese women in Bagan, Burma (Myanmar) work together to hand roll sour plum sugar candies, which they then sell in a street-side business. I traveled through Burma in 2012, just as the country's ruling military junta began to soften its domestic and foreign policies.

Media Case Studies in Ethics

Kony 2012

Look no further than the Kony 2012 campaign for an example of one man's solution being inappropriate for the situation. Kony 2012 was a well orchestrated campaign imploring the international community to step up and demand that world leaders search for and imprison Joseph Kony for his crimes against humanity in Uganda. Kony has perpetrated countless horrors over the span of decades: that is a fact. But if you ask many Ugandans—the ones directly affected by Kony's actions—they are more apt to point out that all of this publicity, outcry, and ultimately financial support from concerned citizens could have been better used to fund education.

People donated because the message and marketing struck a chord. But, understand that there are countless NGOs and organizations working on the ground in Uganda to rebuild the country. These organizations train locals in various trades, build a stronger infrastructure, and work to educate the country's children. Kony 2012, on the other hand, was one man's mission and personal agenda. There is strong international debate about whether the funds he raised to "find and imprison Kony" could have been better used in other areas such as health, education, and social development.

Three Cups of Tea

This case actually made me a bit sad, because the book *Three Cups of Tea* by Greg Mortensen is a wonderful and moving read. I thoroughly enjoyed the book back in 2008. And in 2011, I was disappointed to learn that some of the book seemed to be false. Upon investigation, it became clear that Mortensen's organization, the Central Asia Institute, fell into the trap facing many development and aid groups: follow-through is infinitely harder than the initial push.

Mortensen spent years constructing more than 140 schools to bring education to rural regions of Pakistan and Afghanistan. He gained international press attention and received countless donations to support his efforts. However, a 2011 investigation by the US television program *60 Minutes* found many of his schools empty, unused, and lacking any support from the NGO or the state governments. Mortensen didn't have the experience or community support he needed to make these schools a long-term and sustainable solution. Building the school was just one step. Finding and funding local teachers, affording supplies, and empowering the community to support education was the real issue here.

What Can We Learn From These?

The bottom line: some projects are developed *for* locals, instead of *with* locals.

Your task is to find organizations working *with* local communities over a long period of time.

Shannon O'Donnell

CHOOSING THE RIGHT EXPERIENCE

Finding the right volunteer experience is the hard part. So, let's figure out which type of volunteering is right for your expectations, how you can give back in other ways, and the factors impacting which type of experience you should choose.

Identifying the Volunteer Landscape

Throughout my travels, I have found that volunteering experiences fall roughly into three categories: organized tours, experiences organized by volunteer placement facilitators (middlemen), and independently arranged opportunities. Volunteering through faith-based organizations is a very popular option. When you're researching, know that short-term trips organized by religious groups often fall within the same spectrum of pros and cons as organized tours, while long-term volunteering with them may work more like an internship. Note that, for accuracy, I offer an online bonus cost comparison chart with the sample fees for each category, updated annually: *blog.grassrootsvolunteering.org/vth/*

Organized Tours

Growth in the travel and volunteer sectors over the past decade allowed numerous voluntourism companies to launch. These companies cater to tourists seeking well-coordinated volunteer-oriented tours to various places in the world. But voluntourists go beyond touring the major sights and include elements of service. You may spend as little as ten percent or as much as eighty percent of your trip volunteering on pre-chosen projects. Tour prices range, but since they typically include guides, lodging, and transportation, expect to pay at least as much as traditional vacation tours.

The best voluntour companies have strong ethical guidelines. They meet sustainable tourism standards. They use eco-friendly travel and accommodation when available. Their projects work with the local community toward long-term solutions, rather than creating indefinite volunteer roles. At the heart of it, they cater to socially conscious travelers looking for a short-term vacation with the details handled by someone else.

Middleman

"Middleman" is a catch-all term for placement organizations that facilitate volunteering. And although the meaning of this term, in many contexts, holds negative connotations, I use this positively and in reference to the many ethical placement organizations acting as middlemen for volunteers all over the world. Middlemen are most often organizations that have formed relationships with overseas volunteer projects. Some organizations charge a fee to place you on their own projects that they operate in foreign countries, while another middleman may connect you with an NGO or aid agency working on the ground where you want to volunteer.

The ideal middleman has a clearly defined volunteer fee and provides you with a breakdown of how that fee is used. They give a portion of your placement fee to the organization you're working with. They answer your pre-trip questions, assuage any fears, and help you get directly to your volunteer placement organization once you leave your home country. They provide language and culture classes once you arrive and are willing to help you quickly resolve on-the-ground issues at your volunteer placement.

Independent Companies

At the other end of the spectrum is independent volunteering. The details and research for both traveling and volunteering are handled solely by the volunteer: that means you. This side of the industry is growing rapidly; the Internet has leveled the playing field. Independent organizations are now easily located through regional searches. Volunteers willing to spend upfront time researching and planning the details are able to hand pick a project and ensure that it meets their personal goals and ethical standards. This is an ideal option for long-term travelers, career breakers, families, or interns. Independent volunteers frequently eliminate the middleman by finding low cost and free projects in locations they may already plan to visit.

Know that your independent organization may not cover room and board. Some organizations charge a very small administration fee to train and orient you—if you demand food and board you may be hurting the organization. Free volunteering rarely includes accommodation, but some low cost organizations (with fees under US$500 per month) offer some room and board assistance. They may provide lunch on site, but nothing else, or, perhaps, basic dorm accommodation and a kitchen for your use. What you get for what you pay varies widely, so remember: safety considerations are solely your responsibility when you volunteer independently.

A great independent organization has worked with volunteers in the past, or has a specific niche need at that moment. It works closely within the local community and uses volunteers to supplement and enhance current projects. They openly share their financial structure. The organization clearly outlines what is covered in volunteer fees and has a point person open and enthused to work with international volunteers.

Throughout your company research, also keep in mind that not all organizations are nonprofits. Some other types of organizations include: S-Corps, B-Corps, for-profits, and non-governmental organizations (NGOs) just to name a few.

Expectations for Organized Versus Independent Experiences

Element	Organized	Independent
Transportation	Usually all inclusive: • airport pickup • some sightseeing • arrangements to and from the volunteer placement	Assistance varies widely: • Get yourself to placement, or nearest city. • Arrive each day yourself, if not staying on-site.
Room and Board	Lodging throughout the placement or tour is typically included. Your organization will specifically outline how many meals are covered each day—often most are covered.	Often, room and board are not included in free independent volunteering. Those charging nominal fees may provide something basic. Many will give you tips on local accommodation and affordable local foods. It can vary widely so ask ahead.
Expectations	Volunteer duties are precisely defined. Tasks and volunteer expectations are clearly communicated before you leave home.	Tasks can fluctuate. Some organizations include precise volunteer expectations. Others encourage self-motivated projects with only moderate direction.

Element	Organized	Independent
Tourism	Highlights of the country are a part of the tour. Often includes a guide, history and ample information. Middlemen differ slightly, but usually provide a city tour and local language lesson before the placement.	Will provide ample tourist information. Usually allow weekends for volunteers to travel together to nearby cities and tourism hot-spots. Volunteers use it as a base for independently exploring the region.
Length	Varies widely. Most tours have short week/weekend integration with projects and social enterprises and fit into 5-30 day trips. Middlemen can facilitate short and long-term placements with the "touring" only done on arrival.	Varies widely. Independent companies may take day labor, weekend help, and even placements of six months or more. It's usually easy to extend your volunteering experience when you've arranged it independently.
Point of Contact	Organizations and middlemen are often very connected to the Internet, phone, and Western styles of communication. You will have local and foreign points of contacts and a clear system for getting help if something goes wrong.	Some organizations are incredibly well connected, others are quite remote. There might be just one English speaking contact, or many. You are responsible for asking questions and assessing the level of assistance they can provide.
Impact	Short volunteering stints are not banking on the impact of a single volunteer. They are structured to accumulate the service of hundreds of volunteers toward a social goal. The bottom line? You may see very little progress on a project since you are one tiny piece of the puzzle.	The same theory applies to short independent projects. The strength in independent volunteering is the ability to see a project through to the end, which may mean weeks, months, or years of support (locally and once back home).

Element	Organized	Independent
Ethical Considerations	Corporate structures can have higher overheads, administration fees and tour expenses. Only a portion of your fee is going to the volunteer organization. Consider how the company picks projects, how long they have worked in a community, and what sort of oversight and impact assessments they conduct.	You pay any fees directly to the organization. Organizational structures vary so ask for the breakdown of how fees are allocated. Ask questions about community involvement and the organization's long-term relationship with the projects.
Costs	You pay for a high level of assistance; someone else takes care of the details. The more you pay, the more facilitation and "tour" you traditionally get from the organization.	Many independent organizations all over the world accept volunteers for free in exchange for service, or for nominal fees covering room and board.

Biggest Advantages and Disadvantages of Organized and Independent Volunteering

	Organized	Independent
Biggest Advantage	Everything is taken care of for you, logistically and on the research side. Your middleman or tour operator will match you with a project/placement.	All the money you pay goes directly to the organization. You also typically control more of the volunteer experience, projects, time, and additional travel.
Biggest Disadvantage	More expensive and only a percentage of your fee goes to the host organization. It can also lack a "local" feeling if it's over-organized.	Much more research involved and it might take longer to match yourself with an organization that fits with your ideals and values.

Organized Voluntours Are Right for Some Travelers

Michaela Potter volunteered through a voluntour company. She wrote this interview herself, and it is reprinted here with her permission from MeetPlanGo.com."

When I decided to take a career break in the summer of 2006, I knew I wanted to include volunteering in my experience. There were many factors I considered that helped me decide what program was best for me.

Where did I want to volunteer?

For a while, Peru had tugged at my heartstrings, yet I wasn't completely sold on the idea of spending my career break there. I had visited other parts of Central and South America, but had never been to Africa. After some research, I realized that the heart doesn't lie, and it belonged in Peru. Why else would I have spent the prior year reading up on the Incan civilization, eating ceviche as much as possible, and enrolling in Spanish classes?

What did I want to get out of the experience?

I had pinpointed the type of work I wanted to do, but what else was I looking for? I spent most of my travels hopscotching across countries and continents, so I was looking forward to remaining in one place – Cusco, Peru. Still, I wanted to be able to explore the area and hike the Inca Trail to Machu Picchu. I also wanted the opportunity to practice my Spanish. A cultural experience was also high on my list.

What type of organization did I want?

Given that I was going to be in Cusco for just six weeks, I didn't think I would have the time to make the inroads I would need to find a grassroots organization, plus worry about accommodation. Yet I still wanted a smaller organization that had their roots on a local level but offered volunteer support.

About my volunteer experience with Peru's Challenge

Peru's Challenge is a local organization based outside of Cusco that works with local communities on sustainable projects. Because one of its founders is from Peru, the organization understands the needs of the community. And because the other founder is from Australia, they also understand the needs and expectations of western volunteers.

I worked with the people of Pumamarca, a community whose members survive on their own agricultural products, but receive no support from the Peruvian Department of Education. We helped renovate the school, taught art and gym classes, and worked with the women's group.

I was also able to put my photography skills to use. I photographed the children of the community and helped design a fundraising calendar. Funds raised went toward an emergency medical fund for the village.

In addition to meeting my "what can I do?" needs, Peru's Challenge also fulfilled my "what do I want to get out of it?" needs. Their program fee included group housing for me and my fellow volunteers (we did our own shopping and cooking) and great cultural activities, including Spanish, cooking, and dancing lessons. They also offered several tours of the area and organized my Inca Trail trek.

My experience was fulfilling on every level and I attribute that to the thought and research I put in beforehand.

With her precise desires for a volunteer experience and specific knowledge that she wanted to volunteer in Peru, Michaela was able to navigate the vast number of organizations and find one that fit her needs.

The children in Pumamarca, Peru patiently lined up in preparation for outdoor games during gym class.[12]

An Independent Teaching Experience in Thailand

When I left to travel through Southeast Asia with my niece Ana, I intended to find local volunteer opportunities for the two of us, but I was unsure about the family volunteering aspect. Ana was just eleven years old, and I knew little about family volunteering.

After my first volunteer experience in Nepal through a middleman, I have always arranged volunteering through grassroots organizations that I have found as I traveled. I suspected I could use the same methods to find an independent experience while traveling with my niece, but in the fall of 2011— as we headed to Asia together for the first time—it was the great unknown.

Ana and I based ourselves in Chiang Mai, Thailand, a small city rich with Thailand's northern cultural heritage. From there we had easy access to Burma, Laos and Cambodia for visits, but the bulk of our six months would be spent living in Chiang Mai. For this reason, arranging independent volunteering was my first choice, as I knew I had the time to find and vet local projects.

I found my connection to several independent organizations through a social justice fair I saw advertised at a local coffee shop. At the fair, I connected with Meaghan, the volunteer coordinator for a women's empowerment organization. I explained that my niece and I wanted to jointly spend our time giving back on a weekly basis in Chiang Mai and Meaghan told me more about her organization.

We Women Foundation's mission is to support education, gender equality, and empowerment of non-recognized refugee women from Burma. Chiang Mai has a large refugee community, women and men who have fled over the Burmese-Thai border in hopes of finding opportunity, education, and safety. The organization typically pairs volunteers with refugees who simply need to fine-tune their English language skills so they can pass university entrance exams.

With Ana being just a child, Meaghan wasn't sure her English was "correct enough" to tutor at the university level, but we exchanged contact information and she told me she would ask around for other suitable volunteer opportunities.

A few weeks later, Meaghan e-mailed with good news. One of the Burmese women in the community had a keen desire to learn English, but no previous experience. Aye* was a refugee from the Shan state in Burma who lived in Chiang Mai. Meaghan told her about Ana and me, and Aye was enthused to work with both of us for five hours a week.

Throughout the rest of our time in Thailand, Ana and I worked with Aye twice a week. She started with nearly zero spoken English. Months later, though, as we said our goodbyes, Aye told my niece, in her careful, clear voice, "Thank you very much Little Teacher for teaching me, I will miss you."

I left We Women with a personal relationship with the organization and an understanding of their funding models and how they support the local community. My niece was able to regularly give time and serve while also completing her school work each week.

It felt like a perfect fit, and that's one of the things I love about independent volunteering. Several factors allowed us to enjoy our time working with We Women. We had a flexible time schedule and teaching English was ideal because we could make a lot of identifiable progress over a six-month period. We asked within the local nonprofit community for project recommendations and found out directly from the community where we could best help. Then, I was able to assess our joint skill set as a team and find an organization open to working with children. I had already found an apartment in Chiang Mai, and was comfortable living without food and housing support from an organization. These factors combined into a cohesive and independent volunteer experience that cost me only the time and effort of research.

Because the experience was arranged independently, in the weeks before Ana and I left Thailand, I communicated with my fellow expatriates in the city and found another volunteer who took over teaching Aye. Aye had a strong drive and passion to learn English so she could find higher paying work in the future; her dedication over those six months was an inspiration to both of us.

Aye's name was changed in this story for her privacy.

Aye eagerly practiced speaking and writing English each week at the We Women office in Chiang Mai, Thailand.

How Long Should You Volunteer?

How long you volunteer for is entirely personal, but your time commitment has a large effect on which type of volunteering is right for you.

Got a day?
Short vacations for those with just a day or two of service are often a part of organized tours. Or, practice social tourism on your independent trip by supporting grassroots businesses, cafes, artists, social enterprises and locally-run or community-organized day tours. Remember, you can't do much in a day, but there are single-day opportunities that contribute to a total cumulative benefit when picked wisely and when they keep the issues of dependency and dignity in mind.

Got a week?
Find a service-based tour operator that focuses a week of your trip on volunteering. Or, go independent and arrange a week of service directly through an organization near your vacation spot—you could even make volunteering your entire vacation. Either option works!

Got a month?
Consider finding an independent organization in your field of interest. With a month at your disposal you have time to self-arrange the tourism side of travel and can often save a lot of money by skipping the middleman. Or go through a middleman for a hassle-free, all details handled volunteer trip.

Got a summer or more?
Go independent. Placement fees charged by middlemen can stack up. Long-term volunteers and interns have time to figure out the specific placement details through research or while on the ground. With time on your hands you may find independent grassroots organizations can offer plenty of assistance and you won't need placement organizations.

Got a year?
Consider using the term "internship" when searching for organizations to fit your needs. There are many wonderful companies offering low cost or free placement help for volunteers with a long-term time commitment to give to important projects. I highly recommend long-term volunteering: it's the best way to integrate, understand, and make a difference.

Cambodia's History Through the Circus

The acrobat wrapped her toes around the string of her bow, prepping the arrow. The flexible young woman leading her circus troupe took a dramatic pause to allow the audience to take a collective breath of anticipation as the tension mounted. In the flash of a second her arrow pierced the balloon. The circus had spent two hours telling the story of Cambodia's sad and bloody past. By popping the balloon, she had symbolically eliminated the evil forces and death brought about by the Khmer Rouge that reigned over Cambodia during the 1970s.

The circus was in town, but it was no ordinary traveling circus. My niece Ana and I followed our instincts one afternoon after seeing a faded, full-color advertisement for Phare Ponleu Selpak (phareps.org), a local circus performed by teens and young adults. Our travel dates exactly aligned with one of the circus troupe's weekly shows in Battambang, Cambodia, so we booked an evening performance. Phare Ponleu Selpak is a children's art center in rural Cambodia. At the organization's core is a mission to use artistic practice and arts-based community development to support former refugees. The organization goes a step further, though, and welcomes hundreds of local children into the arts compound every afternoon. The children engage in a variety of arts education channels aimed at teaching them their country's recent history while providing opportunities for them to express themselves and their country's history through art.

In practice, this means that this non-governmental organization operates as a social enterprise. Phare Ponleu Selpak has a strong social mission built into its structure and foundation, but the commercial side of the organization operates like a business, selling tickets to the shows and funneling that money back into their social mission. Phare Ponleu Slepak uses local and foreign aid —alongside immense community input—to teach circus skills, drawing, and painting to any willing child in the community, and sells tickets to tourists passing through town to support these activities.

By the middle of the circus performance, Ana was watching the stage with rapt attention. She didn't fully realize that alongside this blended show of circus skills, music, and art, the haunting storyline told of Cambodia's sad past and all-too-recent genocide. Around us, the raised metal seats were filled with other tourists equally engaged in the performance. Beyond the "official" seats, locals had filled in every available gap—entrance is free for local Cambodians—with their children watching from laps, blankets, and their parents' shoulders. Everyone was mesmerized.

There were deeply serious moments throughout the circus performance. The young acrobats simulated the bloody five years that the Khmer Rouge ruled the country. Then, they showed lighter moments of jaw-droppingly good circus skills.

As the show came to a close, the host for the evening explained more about the organization's mission, its work, and how the performance we'd watched was about to tour Europe in the coming week.

I loved the performance. It broke my heart, but I loved it. The young adults showed incredible, well-honed talent. But more than that, the performance clearly showed that the organization's social mission over nearly twenty years of development work in that community had paid off. I didn't volunteer with my niece in Battambang as time was scarce, so Ana and I instead agreed that we would find cafes run by the local NGOs to do our fair part. Phare Ponleu Selpak is an example of how you can directly support local grassroots organizations and social enterprises when volunteering is not practical.

Finding the circus, though, gave us more than we had imagined. We hadn't counted on finding a tiny community compound filled with love. An organization with a clear mission twenty years ago forged an effective relationship with the local community to jointly address and express their unique needs.

Although I don't have a lot of muscle, or building skills for that matter, Habitat for Humanity welcomed me with projects throughout the day that were appropriate for my skill level.

Match Your Skills with Volunteering

All right, you know what's out there now, and the wide differences between companies, so it's time to choose the type of experience that interests you: teaching, conservation, medical, disaster relief, etc. Jot down a running list as you read through these questions so you can narrow down your ideal experience.

What skills do you possess?
Volunteer experiences run the gamut from skilled to unskilled. If you're a medical student, it may be a no-brainer to find an experience based around health and nutrition. For others, your skills may be strong arms and an able body for hard labor on a conservation or disaster relief project, or perhaps the specialized ability to work with a new organization developing a marketing plan. Look deeply into yourself; you may have skills you don't even realize are valuable.

No one should walk away from this question thinking "I have nothing to offer." Native English speakers can be invaluable in teaching internationally. Even if you sit at a desk each day, consider volunteering your manual labor abilities; domestically and internationally there are projects that simply need a willing hand (even an untrained hand) to construct houses, or reforest national parks. Your strength and willingness are your skills. If you're skilled with Facebook, Pinterest, Twitter, etc, think about how you could lend assistance to the media side of a project—in some cases you can even volunteer your time from home with online-based skills.

What are your passions?
Take stock of what you're passionate about. Are you part of the green movement and interested in sustainable agriculture? Find an organization that matches that interest. Perhaps you love animals and are keen to work with animal shelters. There are organizations to fit a wide range of interests and passions all over the world.

As a volunteer, I often feel more satisfied with my service projects when they are directly connected to a cause or situation that is meaningful in my life.

My local nonprofit hospice organization gave years of service and care to my grandmother as she slowly died of old age and needed nurses and support; in return, I often manage their online data input at events (one of my technical skills that sometimes seems out of place in conventional volunteering, but here there is a need!). Look at the organizations you may already use in your life—many of these have foundations and a nonprofit arm you can volunteer with as a way to give back and further support their work.

Where do you want to go?

Both domestic and international volunteering have similar considerations in terms of weather, seasonal projects, and need-based response (like disaster relief work). If you plan to travel internationally, take stock of the unique social and environmental landscape of the country or region you're visiting.

If you're visiting a recent disaster location, that could make up your mind. Then you just need to decide on a worthy organization. Similarly, visiting a region in the summer versus winter months may narrow down your options for conservation and nature-based volunteering.

Where you volunteer means which region and country. But also consider the environment. Do you prefer urban development projects, or do you really dream of volunteering on a rural farm? Similarly, if one of your volunteer motivations was to learn a language, then your location presents some limitations on that front.

You can think of this in another way: if you know you want to volunteer in Guatemala, but are open to a range of volunteer projects, then you are in a different situation than a volunteer who is willing to go anywhere in South America, as long as they can work in animal conservation. Each of these requires different research methods. Ask yourself where you want to go and then marry that with the passions you just finished brainstorming.

What feels right for you?

For many, the costs of traveling add up and that means your volunteer experience is an investment of both time and money. Find a way to match something that interests you with local needs.

Lee explained how to properly harvest the ripe coffee cherries before he set me, and others on the tour, loose on his village's coffee fields in Northern Thailand.

A Morning with Monks Teaching English

My niece Ana was eleven years old when we traveled throughout Southeast Asia for six months, homeschooling on the road. We incorporated both short and long-term volunteering experiences into our travels and she shared her travel experiences at ALittleAdriftJr.com.

When I was in Luang Prabang, Laos traveling with my aunt, we went to an organization called Big Brother Mouse (bigbrothermouse.com). This is a bookstore that gives out new books, written in Laotian, to kids all over Laos so that they will have something to read (sometimes the ones they give out are the first books a kid has ever seen. I can't imagine!). At the Big Brother Mouse bookstore, every morning they use the shop to teach people English who can't speak it very well. If you speak English fluently, and you're in the city, you can volunteer for one or two hours in the morning to teach people who can only speak a bit.

The first person at the bookshop the morning I went was a monk; he was 19 years old and, of course, he had all of his hair shaved off and was wearing a bright orange robe. He is the one I started talking to and helping. He had a notebook with him full of English words he didn't know how to pronounce, but he had heard someone say them so he wrote them down to ask when he came for his morning practice at the bookshop.

Once we started, my Aunt Shannon and I would say the word to the monk and he would repeat it back to us slowly and cautiously as he sounded out the words and letters exactly how we said them. He had small words like cheap, sleep, sheep and leap. He also had some words that didn't exist and we didn't tell him they weren't real words, we just told him the sound of the letters since he was working on pronunciation.

Soon, a bunch of other Laotian people came in and wanted to talk with us. They were all teenagers and young adult boys. My aunt and I were the only English speakers at the bookshop that morning (thank goodness we went!), so my aunt took half the group and I worked with half the group and we split up and talked to them.

After the boys sat down at our long table, they introduced themselves and I introduced myself (the monk was still there, so he introduced himself too). Then, we started talking about English words they didn't understand and things they couldn't pronounce. All of them spoke English pretty well. Well, well enough that you could have a full conversation with them, but not enough to talk politics, as my Aunt would say, or about anything really big.

The monk had trouble saying the "th" sound because in Laos, they don't make that sound, so I showed him how you bite your tongue and then blow air through your teeth. Only about half of the time he got the sound, but it's better than nothing and he said he would keep practicing once he left.

I want to become a teacher when I grow up, and now that I have taught people how to speak English, I think teaching is a little difficult, especially when teaching something people aren't totally used to learning. Teaching people how to speak English was neat and I hope that I can do it again because it makes me really happy and I feel like I'm heading toward my goal of becoming a teacher. When I worked with the people that day, each one of them was so interested in learning. We laughed so much, and they tried hard to learn and asked a lot of questions since they only have free native English speakers once a day.

Most of the Laotians I taught that day want to have jobs in tourism, so they need to know English for tourists. So, I felt that just giving an hour of my time while I was traveling was easy, and when other people go to Luang Prabang and give an hour of their time, that time adds up and we can all really help these people for a long time.

Ana's story shows that there are service-based learning opportunities for children too. Families can serve their local communities, or serve during international travel, and take away lasting lessons. We'll cover family volunteering later in this section.

The beautiful, gilded Vat Ho Pha Bang in Luang Prabang, Laos.

Choosing a Company or Organization

There is no shortage of voluntour companies and placement organizations, just as there is no shortage of independent opportunities. Sussing out which are worth your time is the difficult part. At this point, you have answered these questions:

- Is my trip ideal for supporting volunteering or social enterprises?
- Am I looking for a full voluntour, a volunteer placement service (middleman), or an independent organization?
- What am I interested in and passionate about supporting through volunteering and socially responsible and sustainable travel?

In the resources section you'll find a list of organizations. Use this list as a starting point for each of the three types of volunteering so you can begin searching for well-suited opportunities. Use the company's website, read the organization's information, research what others have said about them and send them an e-mail if they don't have a handy guide to the information you need to know.

Organizations will have differing application and screening processes for volunteers. Before you apply, evaluate whether you are a good volunteer candidate for that specific organization. Think about matching your skill set, values, time commitment, and interests. It can be tough and competitive to get accepted into some volunteer programs—these organizations need to be picky to ensure that they get a good volunteer.

Knowing the right questions to ask your volunteer organization may seem daunting. You want to ensure that you ask very specific questions that cover each aspect: the company, the fees, tax deduction potential, your safety, the experience, and the details. As a bonus, I offer a very specific, detailed list of questions you can tailor to your circumstance, as well as a sample e-mail, at: *blog.grassrootsvolunteering.org/vth/*

A Conversation with Caroline: An Organization Working for Long-Term Solutions

Caroline Boudreaux is the founder of The Miracle Foundation (miraclefoundation. org), a nonprofit organization that works to empower all orphans to reach their full potential. She graciously offered to let me quiz her on her organization's mission and methodology for working in India. Her organization accepts donations, runs tours for donors, and does not place Western volunteers at the orphanages they support. I wanted to know why.

Caroline, how does your organization find and vet the orphanages you work with in India?

We have a methodology, it's called the NEST, and it stands for Nurture, Empower, Strengthen and Transform. We nurture and empower the staff and the children, strengthen an orphanage's processes and operational procedures, and help to ultimately transform the institutions into loving homes where the children and staff can thrive.

We work with local governments and our staff in India to identify and locate orphanages. We also have a large group of the diaspora of Indians living in America and Europe giving us leads to rural orphanages they know of that are doing the right thing but don't have the resources to provide the children with even the basics.

How long do the orphanages work with you?

It varies by orphanage. We start with qualification and an independent accounting firm checks the orphanage's financing, licenses, and governance structure. Then, the social work audit is based on the Convention on the Rights of the Child as written by the United Nations; the social worker measures how well the orphanage is meeting the child's rights already, before we step in to help.

After passing qualification, incubation lasts between nine months and two years. We identify the gaps—where are the children and staff suffering the most? Usually it's health care, so we work with them to build a project plan to overcome these battles, measuring results every step of the way.

After about nine months, we really know the lay of the land with this orphanage and if they have the best interests of the child at heart. At that point we either certify them or not. If they're certified, then we continue to fund the orphanage; we'll stay with them forever. If they're not certified, and have not worked the program that we agreed to, then we have no choice but to leave the place. We leave them with children inoculated, house mothers trained, clean water systems in place, and a road map for how they can improve, but we don't continue working with or financially supporting that orphanage.

So you have a long-term plan to work with the certified orphanages and maintain support?

Exactly, and it's scalable. We can support, mentor and monitor many orphanages because they are already on the ground and operating. Our plan is to reach eight million children in the next ten years, which represents 30 percent of the children living in orphanages in India. Thirty percent is typically the tipping point. If we help 30 percent of the orphanages run efficiently and effectively, and give children the quality of life they deserve, then the chance of the rest of them running this way is much, much greater.

You run tours to your orphanages in India. What made the Miracle Foundation choose this method rather than volunteer placement?

Running a nonprofit for 12 years now, I can tell you that volunteers are fantastic, but they are hard to manage. If I'm working with a volunteer then I am not doing my job, I am training a volunteer how to do that job. With the tours, we want our donors to meet the children and experience our work firsthand. It's another way we prove our transparency and effectiveness. The groups visit the children and are given a project that will leave that orphanage better than when they found it, so we'll perhaps build a fully finished playground.

And it's so much fun for the children; people come and they have this new fresh perspective and worldview. When we first work with an orphanage, typically every child wants to be a teacher or a social worker. And then, a year later, after a few tours have gone through, the kids say "I'm going to be a photojournalist," or "I'm going to be a doctor."

They open up each other's worlds.

You emphasized finished projects. Have you seen a lot of unfinished projects in voluntourism?
Oh yes, people want to help, but they can only give two weeks or five days. The reality is that you can't really make a lasting difference in the orphanages with that kind of time. Sometimes with voluntourism travel, the winners are the people who travel. And the people the volunteers visit often end up worse for it.

I have seen projects that destroyed the landscape for an orphanage; the children have half a playscape, they have a swing set with no swings and less open space in which to run and play. The organizations simply abandon the project after volunteers leave. And oftentimes, the volunteer even paid to do this project that didn't get finished. I have seen horrific examples of what happens when good-hearted people pay an organization and end up in a foreign country left to fend for themselves.

I really love how transparent the Miracle Foundation is with their financials. That's an important part of this type of work, knowing where the money goes.
Yes, we are very open about our numbers. Perhaps my best tip for volunteers researching a company is to follow the dollar. How much is the organization charging? How much does the project cost? The organization should be willing to itemize every aspect of your fee or donation when you travel with or for them.

Thank you so much, Caroline. I really respect the way you've structured the Miracle Foundation and the work that you do. Is there anything else you'd like to share with future volunteer travelers?
You know, I think it's great for people to want to go over and see how the other side of the world lives, but I think with that comes a responsibility. If you go,

know that the work is really not on the ground. People think "I am going to go and work on the ground and then I have done my deed."

And that is not true.

Your responsibility once you come back home is to take care of that project and the people you got to know. The work on the ground is the fun stuff. The real work is when you get back, to keep working on their behalf. I see people who go, they see, they get this valuable experience and then they run off and do something else. And it's almost like taking. Support your projects financially once you return home. It's important to share our talent and treasure to make sure we end the suffering NOW.

College Students: Study Abroad and Internships

During my four years attending university, my focus was split in several directions. I volunteered regularly, I studied, and I had the overwhelming desire to travel. It didn't occur to me to combine the three. I attended a summer study abroad program in Italy and looking back on it now, I wish I had incorporated volunteering into my time there. With that in mind, here are a handful of tips for how university students can use study abroad programs as a launching point for service.

Find the right program.
There are countless study abroad programs all over the world. Many universities have a special department to handle studying abroad; check with them. Look into reciprocal programs between your university and another campus somewhere in the world.

Research your specialization or major.
Take what you're studying in school and find a summer internship program abroad—in many cases you can receive course credit for your development work. This is the case for undergraduate, graduate, and even research work.

Look into university organizations.

Research the clubs and organizations on your campus: many include service learning goals. Also consider that faith-based clubs often allow non-members to join on their projects, many of which are non-denominational assistance and volunteering. Ask around, be open-minded.

Think outside the stereotypes.

Many study abroad programs form partnerships between European and North American universities. These places need volunteers too. If your study abroad program does not include service, consider finding time each week to serve the community via Habitat for Humanity (habitat.org), beach clean-ups, or homeless shelters. Service can take place in every environment: developed urban cities, college campuses, and rural developing communities.

Consider going beyond short-term service.

Look into the longer, paid volunteer options and programs available to college graduates. My cousin volunteered with the Peace Corps for two years in Guatemala, then went on to work with AmeriCorps to teach in underserved communities in New York City while gaining her Master's degree. It's an unconventional path of service, but rewarding for many to see the lasting benefits of their work within communities over several years.

In my college years, members of my service fraternity, Phi Sigma Pi, donned goofy costumes at Relay For Life to raise money and awareness for the American Cancer Society.

Highly Specialized Skills-Based Volunteering

We've talked a lot about skills-based volunteering, and that there is a place within the industry for both skilled and unskilled labor. The difference between skilled and unskilled volunteering largely depends on the volunteer project. Skilled labor may come from trained white-collar people like doctors, programmers, or teachers. However, in disaster response, conservation work, or agriculture projects, skilled labor may entail plumbers, carpenters, and botanists working right alongside unskilled laborers willing to lend their time hauling, clearing, lifting, and generally following directions.

One side of volunteering that has a lot of room for growth, however, comes from highly-skilled, niche volunteering. By this I mean specialists with more than ten years experience, like lawyers or accountants who have excelled within their field for decades. Engineers, farmers, and executives also fall into the highly-skilled fields that are often in short supply in developing areas. Both domestic and international organizations deeply need voluntary service from professionals, and there are specialized databases within each field of study.

Specialized volunteering is a wonderful option for midlife career breakers, or seniors interested in passing on their specialized skills to developing communities and projects.

The resources section at the end of the book includes professional and specialized volunteer organizations, so if this is you, consider starting there. Your biggest volunteering impact may be realized by using the skills you've spent decades honing.

A Volunteer Journey Through Latin America

Gareth Leonard actively travels and volunteers throughout Latin America and shares the range of his experiences on Tourist2Townie.com.

What drew you to volunteering during your travels?

I strive to go beyond the backpacker trail to develop relationships and learn about foreign cultures on a more intimate level. With that being said, volunteering is something I've always been passionate about because not only can you immerse yourself in a culture and work with people more personally, but volunteering also provides a platform to directly impact the lives of people who expand yours.

What types of projects have you worked on over the years?

During my travels I volunteered at a Monkey Rescue Center in Puno, Ecuador; spent Christmas at an orphanage in Cusco, Peru; traded room and board for labor at a Hare Krishna retreat outside Lima, Peru; helped build a new plumbing system for a school in Cochabamba, Bolivia; and, most recently, I volunteered in Sucre, Bolivia with an organization called BiblioWorks, which builds and supports libraries within the region.

How did your expectations going into volunteering compare with the reality?

Living and traveling through Latin America over the past few years has taught me that coming into a new endeavor with rigid expectations is never a good thing. The reality of each and every volunteer experience I've had has blown away any expectations I could have laid out in advance. Moving forward, my expectations will inevitably grow because of the incredible memories I've taken away from each project. With that, it's my job to ensure that the reality of each new endeavor is more successful than the last.

How do you find and vet projects before you work on them?

My formula is word of mouth with a splash of research. I decided to volunteer with the Monkey Rescue Center, Hare Krishna Truly Village, and Cusco Orphanage because fellow volunteers I met while traveling through Ecuador and Peru told me what a great experience each program had been for them, and how they helped that specific cause.

Volunteering with the BiblioWorks organization, however, was much more strategic. I have a strong passion for literacy and I knew I wanted to volunteer in Bolivia, so I researched and contacted different literacy organizations until I found the one that would be mutually beneficial.

How has volunteering changed the way you see the countries you visit?
Volunteering gives me the opportunity to interact with people on a local level within the context of their everyday lives. It allows me to absorb the true essence of a place while I attempt to leave a positive and sustainable footprint on the projects I pursue.

How do you maintain a connection and/or continue supporting the organizations you volunteered with once you leave?
I try to keep in contact with past projects through the organization directly, or with the people I worked with. One of the great things about having my travel blog is that I can recommend the volunteer programs I've worked with to other travelers.

In my current project, I am working on bringing Save the Children and the Orphaned Starfish Foundation (which I worked with in Cochabamba) together with BiblioWorks to establish more computer-based learning programs within libraries across Bolivia. In this way, I use my voice to bring different organizations together that I think might have similar, complementary goals and aspirations.

The Art of Long-Term Travel and Volunteering

Travelers on gap years, career breaks, sabbaticals, and round the world trips often look for ways to weave volunteering into their long-term travel lifestyle. There are a wide variety of long-term volunteering options that are often easier for volunteers who have several months to give to a project. Alternatively, long-term travelers can regularly find organizations offering small, niche volunteering opportunities that last just a couple of days, which is ideal for travelers passing through a lot of different places rapidly.

Since long-term travelers have more flexible and open schedules, it's important to balance your pre-trip research and on-the-road research so your time doesn't simply slip by without any volunteering.

Ways to Give Back While Traveling

- Find single-day and weeklong experiences in cities you're passing through. Contribute time toward the organization's larger vision/mission using the sites in the resources section of this book as a starting point.
- Support local businesses (social enterprises) like fair- trade coffee shops, restaurants, handicrafts and local initiatives in each new city.
- Spend two to six months in one spot, and see a project through to completion. Volunteers with specialized skills can often witness pieces of the change they are working toward when they volunteer on longer-term projects.

Using Your Pre-Trip Research

Your pre-trip research should uncover a list of local organizations that interest you before you set off on your trip. Once you're on the road, exchange e-mails with possible placements; tell them about your flexible timing once you get a rough sense of when you'll be there, and they can advise you as to the best season for your volunteering and local festivals you can time with your volunteer stay.

An after-school daycare center for single moms, located in the rural outskirts of Xela, Guatemala, uses volunteers to read with the children and help them with their homework.

Spontaneous Volunteering Experiences on the Road

The key to figuring it out as you go is flexibility. If you fall in love with a city and suddenly want to stay a couple of extra weeks or months to volunteer, look in these spots for potential organizations.

- Check bulletin boards in local tourist cafes.
- Read local city-life newspapers and magazines designed for expatriates (expats).

- Find expat Facebook communities and online forums and ask there.
- Find fair-trade, grassroots shops and ask them.
- Visit organic shops; they are frequently tapped into the volunteer community and can be full of locals.
- Search blogs for tips on what other travelers have found just by looking around.
- Ask questions! Other travelers and locals will happen upon great initiatives that haven't yet made it online.

❝ *I really love a disaster response organization called All Hands (hands.org), and I love how they do things. They're a small, transparent organization and I know that the work I do with them is worthwhile. Most of my volunteering experiences have come from working with All Hands. I worked with them in Bangladesh (cyclone recovery – seven weeks); Gonavies, Haiti (hurricane – five months); Sumatra, Indonesia (earthquake – four months); Leogane, Haiti (earthquake – three months); and Mindanao, the Philippines (flooding – five weeks). The work depends on the type of disaster but generally involves cleanup in the initial stages and building later on. I love the physical aspect of disaster response and being able to see the impact my work has at the end of each day.* **❞**

Kirsty Henderson
NerdyNomad.com

The Family Volunteering Lowdown

Many parents view traveling as a way to expand their child's education while fostering compassion, empathy, humility and consideration. When my family and I made the choice to pull my niece out of school in 2011 so she could travel with me through Southeast Asia, I wanted to show her our tiny place in this big world. I wanted her to see people with their own culture and stories that are so different from ours, yet similar on many levels once we dive under the surface.

As a long-time traveler and volunteer, let me assure you that there are numerous family volunteering opportunities all over the world.

Your dream of volunteering as a family is possible.

Of the major list of possible volunteer topics previously mentioned, many have programs that accept children of various ages. Projects that are often popular with families include:

- animal conservation and advocacy
- teaching English
- conservation and nature projects

The easiest way to know if a project is ideal for family volunteering is to ask the organization. Organizations allowing family volunteers will provide age requirements and the precise nature of the program.

Seven Tips for a Positive Family Experience

Identify mutual passions and interests.
What you think might be an easy fit, might not be the right fit for your entire family. Consider each person's needs and interests and how they can intersect.

Involve your children in the decision.
Talk to your children about why you're volunteering and involve them in choosing an experience. Give children an element of control once you've narrowed down the choices. They'll be more invested in the experience if they feel that they picked it out themselves.

Ask a lot of questions.
Know the organization's age requirements and know why those age restrictions are in place. Self-assess if your children are age appropriate. Find out clear details on what an average volunteer day will look like.

Go in with flexible expectations.
Even with a lot of questions answered, know that things might go wrong. It may turn out differently than you expect, which will give you an opportunity to show your child how to cultivate patience and understanding.

Be responsible for your family's well-being.
Even the best-run family volunteering programs might have holes in their implementation. You know your children best, so if they need naps, communicate that beforehand. Consider picking up snacks for long days, and know how close alternative food sources are for picky eaters.

Stay optimistic.
Parents play a huge role in how children behave and react, so be at your best. For me that means a good night's sleep and frequent meals. In short, maximize your ability to handle anything that crops up with a smile on your face.

Communicate with everyone.
Tell your children about the organization, ask questions, and understand what you're doing, and why you're doing it, at every step. Also, keep your organization apprised of your needs, how the experience is working for you, and any expectations you hold.

In Thailand, a locally run sanctuary for rescued Asian elephants, the Elephant Nature Park, welcomes family volunteers and travelers.

Volunteering Changed my Path in Life

Laura Walker volunteers regularly in Africa and worked in South Africa on sustainable community development programs; she shares her experiences at AWanderingSole.com.

As an adventure traveler and Africa enthusiast, I have volunteered in Kenya and Malawi and worked in development in South Africa. While it can be frustrating and mentally exhausting, I always feel a tugging at my heart to return to sub-Saharan Africa. Despite setbacks, corruption, and cultural aspects I will never truly understand as an outsider, a part of me will always feel tied to the people and the land that exist under the African sun.

My life changed when I met a boy named John. It was my first night in Kenya and I was volunteering at an orphanage that had no running water or electricity. I had graduated college and I took off for what I imagined to be a rugged and exotic summer in Africa. As I sat down to eat my dinner, a bland concoction of rice, potatoes, and cabbage, I was introduced to John, a seventeen-year-old boy who lived nearby my volunteer placement.

That introduction cultivated a very strong friendship and a bond that has endured trials beyond my wildest imagination. I don't want to say something cheesy like, "This boy changed my path in life," except that it's the truest statement I can pen. This teenage boy taught me about true struggles in life. John dropped out of school when he was six-or seven-years-old. His mother was severely diabetic, and the untreated illness left her struggling to walk. For four years he worked in neighbors' fields and did his best to provide his mother and siblings with one meal a day.

When his mother passed away, his older brother took him back to school. John rejoined the first grade when he was twelve-years-old as one of the "big boys" (a reference often used in Africa for older kids who have returned to school). Other village kids made fun of him; they thought it was silly for him to be so old and in the first grade.

Unfortunately, his struggles in life did not stop there, but he has overcome seemingly insurmountable odds. John's desire to learn, and his leadership abilities (illustrated by how well respected he is in his village), led me to devote my future volunteer and fundraising activities to education. I was also motivated to make my next career move into social business.

I am happy to say that John is now at one of the best private boarding schools in the country and performing well. He talks excitedly about his school having hot showers, how much his teachers care about him, and how they get to go swimming on Sundays. I speak with him and his brothers every week, and it still surprises me that I have made such deep connections through a simple volunteer experience.

Through this trip, and two subsequent stays at this orphanage, however, I saw the pitfalls of some volunteer projects. Many orphanages in Africa are set up as businesses, a way to draw in foreign volunteers who donate large sums of money that go into the pockets of the orphanage's owners. At the extreme end, some orphanages host children who aren't even truly orphans. These are the realities that potential volunteers should be aware of when selecting a volunteer project. In Africa, I believe the best thing one can give in volunteering is time and skills; if you want to give money, it's best to make purchases first hand.

The orphanage where I met John is now a place to which I will never return. I endured much heartache when I reported on, and acted to stop, the physical abuse and extreme corruption at the orphanage. Of course, corruption also exists within the government, and it took creative ideas from an organization fighting child abuse in Kenya for us to stop the abuse at the orphanage. While it may sound off-putting, this is an example of how deeply a volunteer experience can change you and become a part of who you are. I had no idea that an initial trip four years ago would lead me to fight child abuse in Kenya and seek justice for a five-year-old boy.

John is not the only person who has impacted my life, and I still keep in touch with people from projects I was a part of in Thailand, Malawi, and South Africa. My family ties have grown to span the oceans that separate us, and I know the value I have added to others' lives through volunteering. Of course, I feel like I have received far more from volunteering than I have been able to give and my life is so much richer for these experiences.

A Quick Look: Should I Just Donate?

At this point your mind might be boggling. How do you choose? Is the company ethical and are the fees justifiable, the work helpful? There is a time and place for every volunteer experience, just as there are situations where a donation is a better option.

In some cases it may make more sense on your trip (particularly if it's short-term) to find a worthy independent organization, learn more about them once you visit the city, and ultimately provide a donation to help them with their mission. You could also fundraise for them once you return home. In that way, you are still actively engaged and you bring your experience and observations to your own friends, family and community.

Also, consider visiting social enterprises during any type of travel. Supporting local, sustainable, and fair-trade businesses throughout your travels is an integral part of socially responsible and sustainable tourism. It's also an incredible way to support the local economy and strengthen the community infrastructure in places where volunteering simply doesn't seem like a good fit.

Finding the "Perfect" Organization

Some volunteer experiences over the years have left me disappointed. Some made me question my decision to volunteer, my true impact, and my volunteer organization's intentions. The volunteering industry is riddled with potholes, but through research you will be one step closer to finding a good fit between your core values and an organization you feel passionate about supporting.

In the 1970s, researchers Horst Rittel and Melvin Webber described some development issues as "wicked problems," or rather complex and messy situations with no clear path to solutions. These issues only get better or worse, but are never completely solved.[12] Ethics, politics, and religion cause divergent opinions on how wicked problems should be solved (think of obesity, poverty, and climate change).

Tame problems, on the other hand, have a clear solution that either works, or does not; tame problems can be fully solved in a reasonable amount of time and they remain solved. Examples of tame problems include putting a man on the Moon or landing the Curiosity rover on Mars. Finding the technology to support space exploration is complex, but there is a clear indication of when the problem is solved.

And though Rittel and Webber studied development issues in the 70s, their theories on development hold strong today. Many modern volunteering projects attempt to solve wicked problems. That means that a "perfect" solution does not exist. When you're researching, it's easy to get bogged down in the imperfections, in the one piece of the organization that doesn't seem to entirely fit with your ideals or preferences.

There will be organizations doing so much good, and 90 percent of their project may fit exactly with your ideals and values. And that other 10 percent?

Well, only you can answer if an organization's structure and solution is good enough.

Final Tips for Picking a Successful Experience

Be flexible.

Do pre-trip organization research.

Do pre-trip cultural research.

Realistically consider your time commitment.

Volunteer within your interests.

Find organizations that align with your core values.

Go with your gut when choosing between independent or organized.

Ask a lot of questions of your organization.

E-mail previous volunteers with specific questions.

Volunteer in a destination you've always dreamed of visiting.

Go where your skills are needed.

Give whatever skills/time/efforts they need when you arrive.

Shannon O'Donnell

WHILE
ON THE ROAD

*Landing at your volunteer placement, you may feel a
combination of wonder and excitement. You may
also experience trepidation and culture shock
because of the unknown, particularly
on your first trip abroad.
This is all normal.*

Culture Shock and Your First Days Abroad

For some volunteers, your placement location is quite different from your home country. And if you've arranged an independent experience, without a middleman or tour, then you have more details to deal with as you settle in. Honestly though, these details can greatly help you overcome culture shock by giving you specific tasks that have to be done those first few days.

If you begin to feel particularly out of your element, you might:
* Find other volunteers and get to know them.
* Explore your new home, the city, and your placement.
* Take personal time in your room to read a book, write in your journal, and generally indulge in down-time.
* Watch a movie on your laptop or listen to music.
* Call home. I find a quick Skype call home to hear familiar voices recalibrates me.
* Sleep. Jet lag can create stress if you've jumped several time zones.
* Drink water. Dehydration after long travel days is common and can make you feel sluggish.
* Ask questions, because knowing the answers and learning all about your new environment can alleviate stress.

Finding Peace at a Romanian Bear Sanctuary

Natasha Chow won a volunteer trip at a conference and she ended up out of her normal travel element working at a bear sanctuary for a week; she blogs at glampacker.com.

I didn't expect to fall in love with Misha. Misha has dark brown eyes, a beautiful deep voice, and enjoys eating sweet buns. He has two distinctive white markings on his neck and fluffy chocolate brown fur. Misha is a rescued brown bear cub.

He was six-months-old when he was rescued from a remote village in Georgia and transported to Romania. I met Misha, and other rescued bears, each with their own heartbreaking stories, on a volunteering adventure at Eastern Europe's largest bear sanctuary.

I ended up at the sanctuary by pure chance, or perhaps fate. Before volunteering in Romania, I had never considered the possibility of combining volunteering and travel. My adventure began at a conference, when I casually threw my business card into a prize draw for a volunteer trip with Oyster Worldwide. I didn't expect to win, let alone to be volunteering at a bear sanctuary five months later.

Romania is home to over 6,000 brown bears. Unfortunately, many bears have been victim to human exploitation and are abused as tourist attractions. The bear sanctuary is run by a dedicated Romanian couple alongside a small team of staff and volunteers.

There was no such thing as a typical day when I volunteered at the sanctuary. Some days I was outside raking and doing maintenance work and other days I was preparing food for the bears.

Seeing the brown bears living a peaceful life, often after years of exploitation, was really amazing. I came in every morning greeting the bears like they were my friends. The bears came right up to the fence, almost as if to say hello

– although I think they were really hoping I had breakfast for them! While I didn't physically interact with the bears at the sanctuary, I still couldn't believe how close I was to them.

The great thing about participating in Oyster's volunteer program was being able to volunteer during the day and explore Brașov and the surrounding area in my time off. I visited Bran Castle, also known as Dracula's Castle, in Transylvania; I toured a spectacular cave near the town of Râșnov; and I saw the "Versailles of Romania," the stunning Peleș Castle in the mountain town of Sinaia.

At the end of my volunteering adventure, I felt a mix of emotions. I was sad to be leaving but I also left happy, knowing that the bears were in safe hands. More importantly, I was glad to be helping to spread the word about the plight of the brown bears and the sanctuary. I was also very inspired by my experience; maybe I'll volunteer at a koala sanctuary back home in Australia.

Natasha had never previously considered volunteering, but working at the sanctuary gave her a grounded base in Romania and a way to explore nearby tourist sights.

The rescued brown bears enjoyed a messy breakfast of fruits and vegetables at the sanctuary in Romania.[14]

The Golden Rule and Other Lessons in Etiquette

I grew up in a fairly large family and my four brothers and I got up to all sorts of shenanigans. Through it all though, my mother stressed the Golden Rule above all other household rules:

Do unto others as you would have them do unto you.

When you're out on your volunteer placement, consider this your key to a positive experience. Respect the country's culture/food/language/land as you would like travelers to respect yours if they visited your home country.

Others say it best, so keep these etiquette lessons in mind whenever you step foot out of your home.

Rudeness is the weak man's imitation of strength.
Eric Hoffer

Don't reserve your best behavior for special occasions. You can't have two sets of manners, two social codes – one for those you admire and want to impress, another for those whom you consider unimportant. You must be the same to all people.
Lillian Eichler Watson

Politeness is to human nature what warmth is to wax.
Arthur Schopenhauer

Man is always inclined to be intolerant towards the thing, or person, he hasn't taken the time adequately to understand.
Robert R. Brown

How to Be the Volunteer from Hell

Demand that everything be just like back home.

Wear revealing clothing in a conservative culture.

Be lazy and unmotivated.

Assume you know the best actions.

Be picky.

Refuse to eat the food.

Wear fancy clothes you can't get dirty.

Argue passionately during all misunderstandings.

Do no pre-trip cultural research.

Constantly criticize, "wow, we'd never do this back home."

Pass out sweets to every local child you meet.

Expect that everything will go according to plan.

Demand that everything go according to plan.

Sulk when nothing goes quite according to plan.

Anticipate that your work alone is saving the world.

Traits of a Good Volunteer

Shows cross-cultural understanding and sensitivity

Gives a flexible time commitment

Follows instructions

Adheres to the cultural dress code

Comes with an open mind and flexible expectations

Exercises patience

Is a self-starter on assigned tasks and projects

Does pre-trip research

Reads local authors or books about the region

Knows about the local culture and the region's history

Attempts to learn some local language

Researches cultural norms

Is curious, patient, passionate, and caring

Helps wherever and however help is needed

A market vendor gives alms to a passing monk at the sunrise market in Hpa-an, Burma.

Cultural Immersion Tips

One of the major reasons to travel is for the cultural exchange. Successful volunteers are those who feel like they were given the opportunity to learn a lot about their volunteer community and the local culture. It's entirely possible to go abroad and then cloister yourself away from the newness and diversity, to take the immersive aspect out of the cultural exchange—but really, what's the fun in that?

During your free time from the volunteer experience, consider these ideas for more robust cultural immersion.

- Aim for a diverse experience: talk to children about their perspective, then head to grandparents for an entirely different end of the spectrum.
- Behave as though you are representing your entire country—because you are.
- Find local events, festivals, plays, and parks—places outside of the major tourist spots.
- Practice the local language often, with gusto, and tackle it with an open willingness to learn from those you meet. (Always carry a notebook to write down new words and phrases.)
- Find classes and activities you can join that are appropriate for the length of your stay. Try cooking classes, weaving lessons, a new sport, or attend religious events.
- Take local transportation; this is truly an icebreaker and leads to new friends, new foods (locals are always passing around snacks, so be sure to bring some fruit or treats to share as well!), and a great story.
- Eat street food and visit local restaurants. Restaurants run by expatriates become hot spots for foreigners (and are great for occasionally recharging and enjoying the comforts of home) but finding delicious local eats is a cultural adventure unto itself.
- Stay offline. The Internet is addictive, but step away from your screen during your off-time to enjoy face time with your new community.

I believe in fully immersing in the travel experience via food, conversation, and living like a local. For regularly updated on-the-road travel tips for volunteers, visit: *ALittleAdrift.com/vth.*

Lessen Your Impact and Leave No Trace Behind

At the heart of sustainable tourism is using tourism as a tool for conservation and poverty alleviation, according to the Global Sustainable Tourism Council. Further, it encourages lessening your negative (sometimes exploitive) impact on the environments and communities you pass through, while optimizing the positive potential for tourism. Keep these tips in mind to be a socially responsible traveler and volunteer.

- **Go overland.** Airplane flights use a lot of fuel and have a high environmental cost, so consider flying to your destination country and then traveling overland to various sights and activities.
- **Use local resources**. Source your food, souvenirs and tours from locals.
- **Put your trash where it belongs.** Many countries lack a strong sanitation and trash infrastructure, but even if the locals dispose of garbage in rivers and mountains, take the extra step to dispose of yours responsibly. And if recycling is available, take that extra step too.
- **Lessen your waste.** Bring a device that allows you to clean your own water instead of buying and disposing of plastic water bottles (I use, and love, my SteriPen). At the very least, bring a water bottle, as many guesthouses and hotels have fill-up stations with filtered water.
- **Spend money.** Tourism dollars are an integral funding source for many governments. By visiting national sites, museums, and tourist spots you are stimulating the local economy. Also, spread your money in different places so that more family-run businesses benefit from the money you spend in the country.
- **Support social enterprises and businesses.** Community-sourced organizations are far better than Western companies. Support their businesses whenever possible by spending your money locally. It's one of the simpler ways to stay responsible at your volunteer placement or while you travel.

Through Akha Ama, an independent coffee shop in Chiang Mai, Thailand that operates as a social enterprise, I joined a small tour group to the Akha village where the shop's owner was born and raised.

Shannon O'Donnell

THE NUTS AND BOLTS OF TRAVEL

The travel aspect of your volunteer trip is entirely separate from choosing your volunteer experience. This section will look what you need to know for the three phases of your trip: before you leave, while you're volunteering, and once you return home.

Before You Leave: Cultural Research

I love learning about our world—discovering the nuances of a new culture, uncovering a new (to me) food, and finding our similarities and differences. These are the unique benefits to international travel. Part of becoming an international ambassador for your country (which you become the moment you step foot on foreign soil) is learning about the places you visit.

To that end, I am a huge proponent of pre-trip reading and research done at my local library and on the Internet. I learn the history of a place, but I also learn about local authors, read personal accounts, memoirs, and famous literature from the country and culture.

Research means soaking up the political history (both present and past), local legends, and the personal journey of the people. It means filling yourself with a breadth of knowledge, as well as cues about cultural norms, behaviors and attitudes, that will help build your cultural sensitivity to the country you're visiting even before you leave home.

Types of books to read:
* historical accounts
* memoirs and autobiographies
* regional geo-political books
* famous authors from the country
* famous literature about the country
* poetry

The true voyage of discovery is not a journey to new places; it is learning to see with new eyes.
Proust

Safety Concerns and Considerations

Research is the starting point for determining where your concerns and considerations about safety should be focused. This process has layers of research involved: at the government level, the cultural level, and the grassroots community level.

Only with all three will you truly understand the scope of personal safety issues involved in traveling and volunteering. Although in past sections I separated environmental volunteering from person-to-person projects, these safety ideas encompass every type of travel and volunteer combination.

Understanding Government Warnings

The United States, Canada, the United Kingdom, and the United Nations all have travel advisories, information, and resources that provide insight for travelers and volunteers. Some of this information is quite alarming. Imagine finding a volunteer program in Laos, then reading the US government site—you might think the whole country is still littered with landmines and unsafe, which is far from the truth. Yes, many landmines exist in rural areas, but Laos is well on the backpacker trail in Southeast Asia and has a tourism infrastructure, that, while small, is in place and usable.

So, are government warnings a waste of time?

Absolutely not. Use these sites listed below, but supplement them with additional information from travelers and new organizations on the ground in this region to find a rounded perspective on the situation.

Where to Find Official Information
The U.S. Department of State (travel.state.gov)

Foreign Affairs and International Trade Canada (voyage.gc.ca)

UK Foreign and Commonwealth Office (fco.gov.uk/en/)

Cultural Cues for Behavior and Social Norms

All potential volunteers should read and study books, stories, and news about their travel destination. For some volunteer placements, you will read about the social norms and know them before leaving. In other cases, take your behavior and social cues from the locals of your gender once you arrive.

For women, this may mean covering your hair before walking around in public. Pay close attention to how much skin is showing. In India, their traditional dress often shows off their bellies, while their cleavage and legs are completely covered.

I have found there are fewer social protocols for men; many developing nations have gender inequality issues though, so you may find the dynamics of relationships between men and women much different than you are used to. Touching a woman outside of your family may be a serious offense, so keep in mind how you touch and interact with women. Observe the behavior cues from the men around you.

For both genders, if you see something that confuses you, explain what you observed to your organization and ask for their interpretation and advice.

Grassroots Level Information

Research and find locals who live in the countries you plan to visit, and ask them for advice. The on-the-ground reality is often very different from the media hype, and even different from stories and articles found online. Ask your volunteer organization about behavior and social norms in advance so that you can better prepare your clothes, attitude, and expectations before you leave home.

The Whole Safety Picture

Combining each of these tiers of information will allow you to see a more complete picture of what your personal safety will look like once you volunteer and travel. Many safety pitfalls can be avoided by learning about the culture and adopting behavior patterns specific to the region.

This is particularly important for women volunteers to understand. In some countries, Western women are conferred male status and many behavior restrictions are lifted. This may not be the case, however, in the country you plan to visit.

For both male and female volunteers, your foreign passport affords you protections that, in many cases, the locals do not have. You may be granted privileges (freedom to move through the country, to practice your religion, to adopt certain behaviors) that are solely intended for tourists. Research before you leave.

Final Thoughts on Your Personal Safety
- Don't do illegal drugs. The repercussions and punishment for illegal drug use are often much more severe than in your home country.
- Local police, and common paths toward safety in Western countries, may be corrupted and unsafe in certain circumstances abroad.
- Internationally, the accepted behavior patterns and interactions between men and women vary greatly. You must research the local culture and understand basic behavioral norms.

Despite the heat, while I traveled in Jordan I wore lightweight clothing that fully covered my skin, as well as a traditional scarf that I respectfully pulled over my hair when I traveled outside of the tourist areas.

Visas: Gaining Entry in Five Easy Tips

1. **Ask your volunteer placement.** Once you know the length of your stay, ask for their advice on tourist, work, or study visas depending on your situation.
2. **Visit the country's embassy website.** Determine which visas apply to your situation and the requirements. Start early in case you need references, or it's particularly tricky.
3. **E-mail the country's embassy in your home country.** An e-mail, phone call, or a visit if you're close is ideal so you can confirm the visa requirements and your eligibility. Explain your situation and ask for confirmation and advice.
4. **Apply early.** Start the process early, but not too early. Some visas limit the length of validity from the date of issue, not the date that you enter the country. In that case, you may need to apply just before you leave. Generally, you will need to include a passport sized photo, your passport, a photocopy of your passport, and a completed application, which is then submitted via e-mail or in person. Lucky volunteers may find out that their country issues a tourist level visa-on-arrival and they will need nothing more than proof of a flight out of the country.
5. **Confirm all the dates.** Once your passport has the visa inside, confirm that all of the dates, names, and information are valid well before you board a plane.

Managing Your Health

Volunteer placements run across a wide range of landscapes, locations, climates, and conditions. As such, your health concerns will often be regionally specific. Take good care of yourself. This is the most important task you have before you, and it's one that can sometimes be tricky in developing nations, out in the wild on conservation projects, and even in urban, inner city environments.

Yes, You Probably Need Shots

Put aside your fear of needles and plan a trip to the travel clinic near you because chances are, you're going to need a handful of vaccines and booster shots before you can safely leave the country.

The Centers for Disease Control and Prevention website (CDC, cdc.gov) lists regional diseases, risks, and health concerns for many countries around the world. This is a great starting point once you have your region of travel pinpointed. The Public Health Agency of Canada website also offers a wealth of information (publichealth.gc.ca). Even with these resources, travelers should still consult travel healthcare specialists.

Common Travel Vaccines

You may need some of these, you may need none. I am not a doctor, and this should not be considered medical advice, but these are some of the commonly recommended travel vaccines:

Hepatitis A
Hepatitis B
Tetanus Booster
Meningococcal (for Meningitis)*
Yellow Fever*
Typhoid (they have both pills and shots)
Influenza
Rabies
Japanese Encephalitis
Cholera

* Some countries require proof of vaccination against these before entry.

To Take or Not: The Skinny on Malaria Medicine

What is Malaria?

Malaria is a mosquito-borne infectious disease. Symptoms include an intermittent and remittent fever caused by a protozoan parasite that invades the red blood cells.

Where are Malaria Risk Regions?

Malaria is widespread in tropical and subtropical regions. Risk zones can change and are often seasonal (depending on the monsoon and dry seasons). Generally, there are malaria warnings in effect for areas of South Asia, Southeast Asia, Africa, Central America, South America, and Oceania.

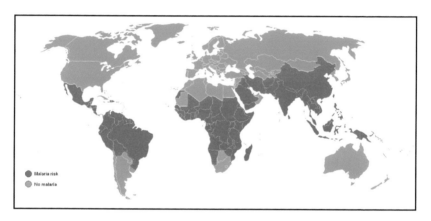

This is a general map of potential malaria risk regions; check the CDC site (cdc.gov/malaria/map) for the latest information.[15]

Types of Malaria Medicines

- Malarone
- Chloroquine
- Doxycycline
- Lariam
- Primaquine

Should You Take Malaria Medicine?

This is a question that should be asked of your travel clinic doctor. They will know which medicines work best in the region of the world that you're visiting. It's also worth contacting your placement organization to find out if they recommend volunteers take the medicine—they are on the ground and have a good understanding of regional risks and potential resistance to the medication in the local mosquitoes.

Your Travel Medical Kit

Packing a good medical kit can solve a lot of minor problems you might encounter in remote and rural placements. In urban placements, you can usually find easy access to local medicine to treat illnesses.

Sample Medical Kit Items:

over-the-counter medicine for diarrhea
antibiotics for more severe traveler's diarrhea
anti-inflammatory medication
general pain or fever reducer
antihistamine
anti-motion sickness medication
epinephrine auto-injector (for those with serious allergies)
bandages of varying sizes
clean syringe (I've never carried one, but have friends who do)
anti-itch cream
anti-bacterial and/or anti-fungal ointment
oral rehydration salts (I highly recommend these; you can replenish them on the road.)
antiseptic wipes
moleskin (for blisters)
first aid quick reference card

Your Prescription Medication

- Carry your original prescription slip and send an electronic copy to yourself in case you lose it.
- Keep the medicine in the original containers.
- Carry enough to get you through, or confirm you can replenish well before you leave.
- Know the generic names for your medication (rxlist.com).
- Many developing countries sell prescription medicine (from the United States/Europe) over the counter without a prescription.

Preventing Malaria

1. Do proper research on the prevalence of malaria in the region of the world that you're visiting. Then ask your placement if they recommend volunteers take malaria medicine, and finish by asking your travel doctor for his recommendation.
2. If you're taking malaria medicine, follow the directions given by your doctor exactly. Some medicines require you to take the pills in advance while others must be taken for several weeks, even after leaving the malaria region.
3. Try to avoid getting bitten by mosquitoes. Even while taking medicine, prevent mosquito bites by using a repellant with DEET, wearing light-colored, long sleeved shirts and pants, and sleeping with a mosquito net.
4. Never miss a dose and never be without your mosquito repellant.
5. Know the symptoms and begin to treat malaria immediately. Symptoms can include chills, headache, fever, nausea, and vomiting.

Insurance: Have Someone Watching Your Back

It's not a sexy topic, but travel insurance is a necessity on all levels. When I travel, I regularly have two types of insurance:
* travel health insurance
* insurance for my belongings

Travel insurance is a broad topic and there is a dizzying array of options on the market. Considerations when researching what's right for your situation include:
* Does your current health and property insurance cover travel?
* Is medical evacuation back to your home country covered?
* What happens to your travel plans and flights during natural disasters?
* Is lost luggage coverage included?
* What sports and activities are included in your coverage?
* Can you access information and submit claims online?

For those packing valuable electronics, consider a separate plan for those items, because most general travel insurance policies have very low-level coverage on your personal possessions.
* What documents will you need to take with you to prove possession? Often you need original receipts before any payouts.
* What level of documentation is needed to prove theft? Understand if you need a police report, photographic evidence, or any other details.
* Confirm that every piece of equipment you intend to insure is allowed within the policy. Certain appliances and electronics may not be covered.

Check out the resources section for a handful of prominent insurance companies.

Managing Your Belongings

The principles of minimalism will serve you well as you plan your trip. Determining what to bring on the road is a huge obstacle for some volunteers, but, by and large, you should know that less is more.

Your Documents

Keeping documents safe tops the list in terms of importance. This is your lifeline, and though documents can be replaced, it is not a pleasant process in any country in the world.

Your passport and travel documents should always be kept in a safe place. In some cases this means carrying them with you, while at other times locking them up at your placement is preferable. Which one of these is ideal for your situation comes down to a judgment call. You're there on the ground; you've done your research and know the local scams, so make the call on where they should be kept.

Also, research local passport requirements because it's often national law that visitors carry their documents on their person at all times. This can often be circumvented by carrying a photocopy with you, but you should ask to be sure.

Scan a copy of all important documents (this means passport, credit cards, vaccinations, visas, etc.) and e-mail a copy to yourself. If you lose your passport, your goal is to have easy access to an electronic copy that you can then show your embassy so you can replace your passport quickly.

The Master has no possessions. The more he does for others, the happier he is. The more he gives to others, the wealthier he is.
From the Tao Te Ching, an ancient Chinese text

Your Money

Variety is the spice of life, or so the saying goes. This proves doubly true for your money. I like a lot of variety in my money when I travel because having safeguards in place, including backup credit cards, has saved me from many hassles.

- Carry different types of cards: MasterCard is ideal in some countries, while others more widely accept Visa.
- Know the fees for international withdrawals on each card. ATM fees add up quickly, so ask your bank about transaction fees before you leave so you can make an educated decision on which to use as your primary card.
- Traveler's checks are very rarely used in travel any more.
- Pack backup cash and one extra card in a separate place from your debit and credit cards. This has saved my hide several times when one card was compromised, and when I traveled to a town without ATMs.
- Exercise caution when you use ATMs. I much prefer well lit ATMs attached to local banks over free-standing machines that can easily be tampered with.
- Call your bank and place a "travel warning" on your card so that the bank does not freeze your card for suspicious international transactions. They will ask you which countries you plan to visit and for how long.

At the end of the day, although it's a hassle and quite stressful, you can get money wired to you through Western Union. My debit card was cloned and compromised in Guatemala in 2010 and this forced me to hunker down for a week and wait for my company to ship a new one. Thankfully, I had the gracious support of my volunteer and language organization. Then, in 2011 my debit card was eaten by an ATM in Thailand, but I had enough backup cash to tide me over until a new one could be shipped to my next country, Jordan. So, in this way, I know firsthand just how tricky it is to get new cards and cash, but I also know that it can be done.

Smart Packing for Volunteers

What items are unique for volunteers? This is one of the questions you'll definitely want to ask your volunteer placement, since it can vary widely depending on the type of service. The clothes you need for camping on a reforestation project in the middle of the winter will be very different from those that you will need while teaching at an inner city school. Examine this list for what may be relevant for your specific niche.

Headlamp: hugely useful for traveling in a broad range of situations.
Medical kit: medicines, bandages, and antibiotic creams at a minimum.
Repellent with DEET: can prevent several types of common illnesses present in developing countries.
Travel adapters: a multi adapter kit to charge electronic devices in different outlets.
Sleep sheet: a silk-cotton blend sleep sheet keeps you in a cocoon of your own cleanliness. This can be very handy since top sheets are uncommon in many countries.
Sarong: multiple uses—this is great for a sheet, scarf, beach cover-up, sun protection on open air transport, etc.
Luggage lock: simple luggage locks deter petty theft. Consider a PacSafe net if you are very concerned about your electronics, as well as a larger lock for lockers if you plan to use hostels.
Spork or utensil combination: it's handy, and oftentimes more sanitary, to have your own cutlery or foldable chopsticks with you.
Sunscreen: I carry a travel-size version in my daypack and a large bottle in my backpack.

For women – reusable menstrual cup: eliminate the worry of your period by carrying a menstrual cup rather than pads and sanitary napkins. I love it, and recommend every woman look into this option.

Other items that depend on your specific placement could include: hat, conservative lightweight clothes, heavy outdoor jacket, camping gear, long skirt for women, pants for men, regionally appropriate swimwear.

Wait, Before You Leave...

Communicate your specific travel details to those at home. Give family members, next of kin, or close friends all the information you have for your volunteer experience. Include the name of the organization, their website, your main contact at the organization, where it is exactly, the dates you plan to be there, and where you plan to travel before and after your volunteering experience.

Give the volunteer organization your information. Include next of kin contact and any allergies, medical issues or special considerations. They may not ask for it, but once you arrive, give it to the person in charge, just in case.

Carry travel insurance. Some voluntours provide this, but everyone traveling abroad should carry travel insurance that includes medevac coverage, repatriation of remains, and hospital care. Also consider a travel policy that insures your electronics, as most travel insurance does not.

Bring a medical kit appropriate for the region where you're traveling. This includes any antibiotics you might need, malaria tablets, an ample supply of prescription medications, and clean needles if necessary. Check the resources section for links to sample travel medical kits and tailor them to your specific trip.

For a bonus "Before You Travel Checklist," visit the travel tips and information page on my site, at *ALittleAdrift.com/vth*.

On the Road: What Happens When Things Go Wrong?

The Boy Scout motto works well. Be prepared.

There is no way to completely anticipate the unexpected in life, but being prepared with a few basic precautions goes a long way. What if you have a family emergency back home, or you fall ill while traveling? Are you prepared if you arrive and have some issues with your volunteer placement?

Safety is one of the big fears for many volunteers when leaving their home country, particularly if it's the first time. International news often errs on the side of sensationalizing negative events, highlighting the aberrations and isolated incidents. There are two sides to safety: personal safety, and the general safety of the countries you visit.

When the Worst Really Did Happen

My first trip outside of the United States was for a study abroad program in Italy while in college. Four days into the program, my brother passed away. I was a new traveler and I had left the US with enthusiasm, but very little meticulous planning. Though I was conscientious enough to leave the contact details for my Italian university with my parents, I forgot to include the city calling code in my list of phone numbers.

This was before rampant Internet use, so I had little e-mail access and my parents spent a very long twenty-four hours contacting my American university (through which I had arranged the study abroad) and then tracking me down to the pensione where I was living.

My carelessness caused undue stress and anxiety for the people forced to track me down. Now, I send my parents e-mail updates on where I will be, when, and any specific, clear details I happen to know. Though the worst has already happened, I'm determined not to put them through that again because of a lack of planning and forethought. E-mailing the details is pretty easy to take care of before you leave.

Resolving Issues and Safety with Your Placement

I cannot stress enough how important flexibility is, not only to volunteering, but to any sort of travel. Patience and flexibility alone can resolve the most common issues volunteers face. So, if an issue crops up, first assess the severity and whether or not you are in danger. If you are not in danger and if the issue is relatively minor (involving tasks, expectations, or adjustment issues) consider communication and flexibility to be your first steps toward resolution.

If you are in danger, however—and volunteer horror stories can happen anywhere in the world—take immediate action to protect yourself. It's a sad fact that some volunteers encounter unsafe, unsanitary and simply unacceptable conditions.

Consider these suggestions so you can take the most appropriate action:

- Trust your instincts and leave immediately if you feel that you are in danger.
- If possible, e-mail, call, or visit your primary contact and explain both the situation, and that you would like them to assist you in leaving.
- For issues that are relatively minor, but are deal breakers for you, consider finishing out the week if it will be difficult for your organization to replace you.
- Do not risk serious health and safety issues for the sake of volunteering.
- If you fall sick, seek out treatment at an appropriate facility. This may mean a hospital or clinic near your placement, or you may need to activate your health insurance plan and be airlifted to a different medical center.
- Be prepared (and willing) to lose any volunteer fees that you had already paid.
- Once you leave, be prepared to organize your own lodging, food, etc.
- In the very worst situations, realize that in some places local police are bribed to overlook certain indiscretions and you are an outsider in the community.

It could be best to cut your losses and leave the town immediately via any available means (bus, taxi, train, or airplane).

Extreme danger on a volunteer placement is rare; it's the exception rather than the rule. Consider that while even credible voluntour trips can go poorly, a lot of major safety issues in the volunteer industry come out of poorly researched independent volunteering experiences. If you choose to volunteer independently, the onus is on you to thoroughly research your housing, food, and the availability of health services so that you arrive ready and empowered with the information you need to take care of your personal safety.

It is easy to get caught up in the idea that you should be willing to sacrifice in order to serve. But there are hard limits, and your safety is one of them. I always travel with a minimum of $100 in "safety" cash and I have $1,000 accessible and set aside in my bank account for emergencies. Before you leave, be mentally prepared to use this money for your safety if you need it. Knowing ahead of time that you have allocated this money for safety will make you more willing to act immediately to protect yourself.

Returning Home: How to Overcome Reverse Culture Shock

Your dream volunteer vacation is over, and you've returned home. Returning to your home culture can sometimes be the biggest shock of all. Research finds that volunteers who easily adapt to their new culture may actually experience more severe reverse culture shock when they come home.

For me, my experiences volunteering were deeply personal, and at times completely immersive and intense. Then, I returned home to a country that had moved on without me. My year abroad distanced me from my home and my friends in a way I couldn't have imagined. I experienced a profound shift in my perspective at my long-term volunteer placement. I felt like I had changed and become a different person. But coming back was a jolt because family and friends interacted in the same manner as before I left.

Common Feelings upon Re-entry

- Overwhelm
- Confusion
- Sadness
- Nostalgia
- Anger
- Depression

You are unique, and culture shock manifests in different ways for different people.

An impromptu cooking class taught how to make traditional Chinese dumplings in Yangshuo, China – my goal was to learn enough to prepare these dumplings once I returned home!

Bring the Experience Home

One of the best ways to settle back into your home culture is to find a way to bring the experience home with you.

Cook for friends. Bond with your friends by hosting a dinner party and preparing some of your favorite new dishes and drinks.

Find a restaurant serving the cuisine. Bond with the chef and staff over the flavors and foods you miss from your time volunteering.

Continue learning the language. Find clubs and cultural associations in your city to continue regularly immersing yourself in the language

Fundraise for your cause. If you love the organization and the work you did, why not host an event to raise funds for the project? By doing so, you help educate your local community about the issues and opportunities in other places in the world.

Communicate with your new friends. Write letters, become Facebook friends, and reminisce with your fellow volunteers and the organization staff to keep the experience alive once you return home.

Find a local live streaming radio station. Keep the music and culture alive through the power of the Internet.

Spend time alone. Go hiking; use your travel skills to explore your hometown in a new way. I guarantee you'll find some things you never noticed before.

Maintain a journal. Record your thoughts and reflect on the experience and what you learned. Writing regularly can help you sort out mixed emotions.

Volunteer. Find a new organization (several great American and European ones are listed in the resources) and volunteer within your local community—there is a lot of need very close to home.

Community Roundup: My One Piece of Advice

I asked past volunteers, current sustainable travelers and people working within the development industry for their one piece of advice for volunteers:

Do your homework. Otherwise, preconceived expectations will only set you up for disappointment. And don't anticipate your work will change the world – in many cases it's more about an honest cultural exchange. **– Michaela Potter**

Get involved with something you truly believe in. The point of volunteering is to have a positive, sustainable impact on the project you're working on, for the greater good of a particular community. **– Gareth Leonard**

Bring a positive attitude and no expectations. Don't come into a volunteering stint expecting to save the world or expecting people in the local community to shower you with praise and thanks. Just come in, work hard, get stuff done, be happy to contribute in some small way, and you'll leave having had a great experience. **– Kirsty Henderson**

Find a cause you believe in and reach out to organizations you trust that are active in that space. Make a personal connection if you can, offer your time, skills, money, ideas or a combination of all of them, and see what happens. You might be amazed where you end up—I know I have been! **– Dave Dean**

It all comes down to respect, and how you respect the culture where you're going. Think about your actions, your behaviors. Respect the local customs and blend in as well as you can. Then take your experience back home and champion that cause. **– Caroline Boudreaux**

I am only one,
But still I am one.
I cannot do everything,
But still I can do something.
And because I cannot do everything,
I will not refuse to do the something that I can do.

- Edward Everett Hale

Go, Give, and Receive by Volunteering

The desire to volunteer and connect, share and hone compassion through service is rooted deep within the human psyche. We crave human connection and as the Internet has opened up the world to us, it has also shed increasing light on the huge inequalities and wealth disparities that exist. On some level, volunteering is a way to appease my soul, to humble myself and give time and service to worthy causes.

Though this book has focused primarily on finding, vetting, preparing for, and successfully partaking in your volunteer experience, I am equally passionate about the idea of supporting local businesses and social enterprises while traveling.

There are many, many ways to work toward a better planet and only you know which areas of service are ideal for you and your situation. If you've gotten this far in the book then you're leaps and bounds closer to making your dream to travel and volunteer a reality.

The moment the idea to travel around the world formed in my mind, I was set on a path that changed me forever. My perspective has grown through travel and my thirst for knowledge-based advocacy has increased.

I have committed to service, committed to travel, and committed to empowering others to find socially responsible ways to travel and serve sustainable organizations all over the world.

Now it's your turn to make that commitment.

Wadi Rum, Jordan.

Travel is more than the seeing of sights; it is a change that
goes on, deep and permanent, in the ideas of living.
Miriam Beard

Shannon O'Donnell

RESOURCES

These resources are a starting point for your research. Search beyond and consider programs and companies not on the list – I simply could not list them all. And though I have looked into each resource listed, companies change over time, so ask your own questions. Also, this list of volunteering resources will be updated with new information and notes bi-annually only for Handbook readers on my site: *blog.grassrootsvolunteering.org/vth/*. Updated travel resources and tips for when you're on the road can be found on my travel blog, at *ALittleAdrift.com/vth*.

Choosing the Right Experience

Independent Volunteering Organization Databases (often full of low-cost opportunities and no middlemen companies)

GrassrootsVolunteering.org – This is one of my sites which offers a community-supported dual database of international independent organizations, as well as local social enterprises all over the world, searchable by experience, location, or duration.

Idealist.org – A very helpful site and a good starting point. Search by family and student opportunities, or location criteria. Be warned, though—some of the listings are middlemen, not independent organizations.

WWOOF.org – World Wide Opportunities on Organic Farms is ideal for farming and agriculture travelers. It requires a small fee for access to their database of global farms that trade farm labor for room and board.

KindMankind.net – A growing database of small, community- run organizations recommended by other travelers.

cie.uci.edu/prospective/iopother/index.shtml – This is the University of California's resource list and has some great options you may not find elsewhere.

VolunteerSouthAmerica.net – The site is very basic, but contains a long list of NGOs needing help throughout South America.

Specialized Skilled Volunteering

CFHI.org – Child Family Health International places health science students on two- to eight-week global health education programs.

CNFA.org – Farmer to farmer programs for those skilled and trained in agriculture.

DoctorsWithoutBorders.org – Accomplished doctors compete to work within this organization. Acceptance is highly competitive.

EWB-usa.org – Engineers Without Borders is a wonderful way for engineers to train and empower communities with a highly useful skill set.

FSVC.org – The Financial Services Volunteer Corps is ideal for professional accountants, financial advisors, and anyone in this specialized niche.

ISLP.org – The International Senior Lawyers Project requires volunteers to have roughly ten years of experience in law.

IESC.org - International Executives Service Corps places volunteers with businesses and projects that benefit from highly experienced leaders.

Kiva.org/fellows - Practical, hands-on experience in microfinance; highly selective long-term programs.

UNV.org –United Nations Volunteers provides competitive and skill-based volunteer opportunities for volunteers from more than 160 countries.

Winrock.org - Skill-based volunteer placements in a wide range of areas (agriculture, business, livestock, gender, governance) for American volunteers all over the world. Competition is high, and programs are funded in partnership with US Aid.

ACDIVOCA.org – Start here if you have a specialized skill that doesn't appear in this list. They offer a wide range of niche projects.

Niche Volunteering (Family, Students, Long-Term)

GenerationOn.org – Domestic US family (kids and teens) volunteering opportunities sorted by zip code.

PeaceCorps.gov – A two-year commitment is mandatory, and the programs are highly selective and offer global placements. Programs are very popular with recent university graduates.

AmeriCorps.gov – Often referred to as the domestic version of the Peace Corps. There are long-term, paid positions serving communities within the United States. Some programs even offer students loan payback or assistance for their service.

ICYE.org – The International Cultural Youth Exchange has some wonderful short and long-term projects for students.

EarthWatch.org – A very neat organization pairing volunteers (including teens and families) with researchers around the world to work on environmental issues. Research volunteer placements are pricey, though.

GlobalCitizenYear.org – Ideal for graduating high school seniors keen on a year of serious study and service.

Domestic Volunteering (North America/Europe/Australia)

UNICEF.org – Volunteer with UNICEF in most Western countries, and they have a great free iPhone app.

Oxfam.org – UK domestic service options.

Govolunteer.com.au - Go Volunteer has options throughout Australia.

Rotary and Kiwanis clubs – If you live permanently in the US, joining one of these clubs can be a great way to give back regularly to your local community.

AmericanHiking.org – Trail building volunteer vacations in the US are ideal for nature lovers.

VolunteerMatch.org – A full and thorough domestic US database of organizations and projects.

Volunteer.ca – A domestic resource for volunteering in Canada.

Volunteering Placements (Middlemen)

GlobalVolunteers.org – This company has been around for a long time, and is well respected. They offer programs for families, seniors, solo travelers, and groups. Volunteer vacations typically last two to three weeks.

ProWorldVolunteers.org – One of the best middlemen options, but on the expensive end of the spectrum. It's highly rated by National Geographic for their work. Community-driven projects and great in-country volunteer support.

GVIUSA.com and GVI.co.uk – A respectable option for volunteer placement and assistance on your trip. They donate some of your fee to the volunteer programs.

CrossCulturalSolutions.org – With listings for teen placements, internships and study abroad, they have some unique options. Fees are on the high end of the spectrum but include travel insurance.

Go-VolunteerAbroad.com - A database of organizations and companies. The results vary in quality but it's a good place to perhaps find some local projects.

Projects-Abroad.org – A huge global organization with extensive experience placing volunteers.

i-to-i.com – None of your program fee goes to the organization, and while that is a major drawback, they are market leaders for voluntourism and stay within communities long-term.

VolunteerHQ.org – Feedback has been consistently positive, they have reasonable fees and are open and honest about the money trail if you ask.

Voluntours

GAdventures.com – Only some of the tours include volunteering, so make sure to choose that search option. They work with Planeterra.org and work long-term with communities.

AfricanImpact.com – Ask a lot of questions about your specific placement. They are well-regarded but I have little experience with the company.

Biosphere-Expeditions.org – Really neat conservation vacations. The company is well respected and offers truly unique tours.

Sites about the Issues in Volunteering

Voluntourism.org – One of my favorite sites. The monthly newsletter always includes wonderful resources and articles.

GSTCouncil.org/blog/ – Read up on sustainable tourism and development. The organization works with the UN Foundation.

TransitionsAbroad.com – A powerful combination of informative newsletter, blog, and volunteer opportunities, as well as a great resource section.

Cultural Research Before Your Placement

ALittleAdrift.com/best-travel-books/ – My travel site lists books by country that are hand-picked as interesting pre-travel reads (includes movies and music as well!).

LonelyPlanet.com – Each country page on the site has a recommended reading section.

UNDP.org – The United Nations Development Programme provides detailed information on various common development issues.

OneWorld.net – A great site with a social mission. Their news headlines aim to help people everywhere understand global problems.

Wikipedia.org – Contains crowd-sourced information and it can be very up-to-date. It offers a digestible version of a country's history and a bit about culture, economics, etc.

Amazon.com – Allows you to search the book section by country and/or topic.

Book Lust: Recommended Reading for Every Mood, Moment, and Reason by Nancy Pearl. Nancy is a librarian who teaches how to pick a book and offers wonderful categorized recommendations on books, authors, and genres.

The Nuts and Bolts of Travel

Health and Vaccinations

Travel.state.gov - Health tips and safety warnings from the US Department of State.

CDC.gov – The Centers for Disease Control and Prevention has updated travel vaccinations lists and resources.

ISTM.org – The International Society of Travel Medicine's global travel clinic directory (under the ISTM Activities) locates trusted travel clinics worldwide.

The Complete Idiot's Guide to Vaccinations by Michael Joseph Smith and Laurie Bouck

How to Shit Around the World: The Art of Staying Clean and Healthy While Traveling by Dr. Jane Wilson-Howarth

RedCrossStore.org and TravelDoc.com – Both offer well-stocked travel medical kits.

Packing

MenstrualCupInfo.wordpress.com – Detailed information about choosing and using a menstrual cup.

ALittleAdrift.com/rtw-travel/ – A list of packing lists from other travelers and volunteers, with links to products and services I recommend.

Insurance Companies

IMGGlobal.com – IMG Patriot insurance is the company I have used and enjoyed while traveling with my niece.

WorldNomads.com – I used this company on my RTW trip. They offer great coverage for backpackers and adventurous travelers and have an active, supportive staff.

Clements.com – Insure your electronics and expensive possessions separately from your travel policy (which likely does not include cameras, computers, etc.)

Other Tips and Resources

XE.com – Check the currency conversions and rates before you get on the flight.

Emergency First Aid & Treatment Guide – This iPhone App has lifesaving tips and advice if you need to respond to an emergency.

Endnotes

[1] Ashley Armstrong, Megan Epler Wood, Ayako Ezaki and Kelly Galask. Voluntourism Guidelines Survey Summary Report, http://www.ecotourism.org/voluntourism-research, (2011).

[2] Tourism Research and Marketing. Volunteer tourism: A global analysis. (2008).

[3] Canadian Centre for Philanthropy, National Survey of Giving, Volunteering and Participating, http://www.givingandvolunteering.ca/files/giving/en/factsheets/benefits_of_volunteering.pdf, (2000).

[4] Musick MA, Wilson J. Volunteering and depression: the role of psychological and social resources in different age groups. Social Science & Medicine. http://www.bidmc.org/YourHealth/HolisticHealth/TravelandHealth.aspx?ChunkID=78992, (2003).

[5] Ariel Garten, The Neuroscience of Conflict, a Big Ideas speech. http://www.channels.com/episodes/show/12970837/Ariel-Garten-on-the-neuroscience-of-conflict, (2007).

[6] Bruno S. Freya, Stephan Meier, Pro-social behavior in a natural setting, http://teaching.ust.hk/~bee/papers/Chew/04Frey-Meier-Pro-social%20behavior%20in%20a%20natural%20setting.pdf, (2003).

[7] Corporation for National and Community Service, Office of Research and Policy Development. The Health Benefits of Volunteering: A Review of Recent Research, http://www.nationalservice.gov/pdf/07_0506_hbr.pdf, (2007).

[8] Sookhan Ho, Volunteer tourism: A tale of two communities, http://www.research.vt.edu/resmag/2009winter/tour.html, (2009).

[9] Monica Pitrelli, Orphanage tourism: help or hindrance?, http://www.telegraph.co.uk/expat/expatlife/9055213/Orphanage-tourism-help-or-hindrance.html, (2012).

[10] Voluntary Service Overseas, The Live Aid Legacy: The developing world through British eyes, http://www.eldis.org/vfile/upload/1/document/0708/DOC1830.pdf, (2002).

[11]Michaela Potter, How to Choose an International Volunteer Program, http://b2b.meetplango. com/2009/03/how-to-choose-an-international-volunteer-program/, (2009).

[12]Photo copyright Michaela Potter.

[13]Australian Public Services Commission, Tackling Wicked Problems, http://www.apsc.gov. au/__data/assets/pdf_file/0005/6386/wickedproblems.pdf, (2007).

[14]Photo copyright Natasha Chow.

[15]Malaria Photo, Creative Commons credit: http://commons.wikimedia.org/wiki/User:Petaholmes

Shannon O'Donnell

Shannon O'Donnell is a writer; she publishes *A Little Adrift* (alittleadrift.com), a travel blog sharing stories, culture, and photography. She also runs her passion project, a community-sourced database of local, sustainable organizations around the world, *Grassroots Volunteering* (grassrootsvolunteering.org). Her story, writing, and photography have been used in *Cosmopolitan Italy*, *BBC Travel*, and *Lonely Planet*, among other publications. Shannon actively travels for the better part of each year and has a home base in Florida.

Shannon O'Donnell

Shannon O'Donnell